What Did I Write?
Beginning Writing Behaviour

Heinemann Educational Books

361 Hanover Street, Portsmouth, NH   03801-3959
39 Rawene Road, Birkenhead, Auckland 1O New Zealand
Halley Court, Jordan Hill, Oxford OX2   8EJ England

ISBN: 0 435 01120 0
       0 86863 250 3 (N.Z.)

Library of Congress Cataloging in Publication Data

Clay, Marie M.
  What Did I Write?

  Bibliography: p.
  Includes index.
    1. Reading (Primary) 2. English language—Writing
3. English language—Study and teaching (Primary)
I. Title
LB1525.C6 1979   372.6'23   79-17088

Set in 11 pt. Optima by City Typesetters, Auckland
Printed in the United States of America by Northeast Offset, Inc., Chelmsford, Mass.

Contents

Here is the Trees
with
house's
byit

1. Introduction

When I observed five year old children very closely during my research on beginning reading I found the early months of schooling crowded with complex learning. Although teachers usually responded sensitively to their pupils' problems there were times when they did not observe the poor responses which might have been leading some children into confusion. How could young teachers sharpen their observation of children's efforts? With the thought that the children's own work samples might tell the clearest tale I began this book. I soon discovered that the messages conveyed by the work samples were as complex as the problems which children face, and I have simply tried to make children's difficulties a little more obvious by organizing the material and annotating the examples of their work.

The particular children who prompted me to write this book were five year olds who entered school in the first two months of the school year. They were children who lived in a city and most of them came from English-speaking homes. When a sample of work has been included from a Chinese or Polynesian child it is used to emphasise the contrast between children who already spoke English well and children for whom English was a second language. Many of the examples were gathered from classrooms, but the most creative were spontaneously produced at home, and were collected by helpful mothers.

The Theme

Instruction in handwriting is NOT the subject of this book.

Nor is the text concerned with pedagogical decisions as to what to teach at which moment and by what procedure. It is a collection of children's work samples with some statements of what they seem to me to imply.

Many of the schools in which observations were made did not place much emphasis on separate lessons in how to print during the first year of formal schooling. The creative urge of the child to write down his own ideas was considered by teachers to be the important thing to be fostered in written language. How did children learn to print? They

- drew pictures and the teacher wrote dictated captions.
- traced over the teacher's script.
- copied captions.
- copied words around the room.
- remembered word forms, and wrote them independently.
- invented (generated) word forms, often correctly.
- got a written copy of unknown words from the teacher.

The teacher gave an occasional group lesson on letter formation, perhaps once a week, and gave daily individual guidance in letter formation.

In schools that did have lessons for forming letters and printing words in addition to daily draw-a-picture and write-a-story activities the pupils did not appear to differ significantly from those in other schools in the skills they gained. The writing syllabus suggested that teachers use an italic script, with slope and an upward turn at the ends of letters; but this was only one model of written language presented to children, as other types of print appeared in their caption books and reading books. However, the italic forms were probably dominant in the children's experience because, when a child dictated a message to the teacher, she wrote it under his drawing in italic script and at that early stage of writing behaviour the child traced or copied this model.

Handwriting is not the theme. What is? As the child discovers that speaking (with which he is familiar) can be conveyed by print he must set himself the task of understanding many arbitrary conventions which we as adults accept so readily. The examples in this book try to illustrate some of the insights that a child gains during his first contacts with written language and some of the points at which he can become confused. His attempts to write tell us something of the things he is noticing in print, although we must always remember that his eye may perceive more than his hand can execute.

A creative writing programme can provide the teacher with an excellent source of evidence of a child's development if the teacher knows what the child was able to do one or two months previously and how his current product can be evaluated against that earlier work. This is easily arranged if the child's work is dated and saved in a folder or book. A comparison of early and later work may show that the child is halted in the process of finding out more and more about the details of print. The observant teacher can then search for further cues to the source of the child's confusion.

The theme of this book is the child's gradual development of a perceptual awareness of those arbitrary customs used in written English. It does not provide a specification of how to teach printing. It tries to make apparent the diverse difficulties faced by individual children. School progress is likely to be halted or hampered by persisting confusions.

Beginning Writing and Beginning Reading

What is the relationship of early writing to early reading? A creative writing programme seems to be the necessary complement of a reading programme which stresses sentences and meaning. The child who engages in creative writing is manipulating the units of written language— letters, words, sentence types— and is likely to be gaining some awareness of how these can be combined to convey unspoken messages. The child is having to perform within the directional constraints that we use in written English. The child is probably learning to generate sentences in a deliberate way, word by word. He makes up sentences which fit both his range of ideas and his written language skills. Fluent oral language may permit the young reader to depend almost entirely on meaning and the eye may overlook the need for discriminating details of letters and words. Creative writing demands that the child pay attention to the details of print. To put his messages down in print he is forced to contruct words, letter by letter, and so he becomes aware of letter features and letter sequences, particularly for the vocabulary which he uses in writing again and again. These words become part of his writing vocabulary, the ones that he knows in every perceptual detail.

Language can be thought of as a hierarchy of units: sentences can be broken down into phrases, phrases into words, and words into sounds. The good reader can work at any of these levels in the hierarchy. The poor reader tends to specialise in words or sounds and may be ignoring the details by which letters are distinguished. But this is not possible in early writing. All features of the language hierarchy must, inevitably, receive attention as the child builds letters into words, words into phrases and phrases into sentences and stories.

Is the child frustrated by the writing task? Observations and examples of work suggest that while the child is discovering letter forms and creating his early messages the task seems to have its own attraction if his efforts have been responded to with appreciation.

Later the verbal child may have many things to say and

Natasha to mother: What does this say?
Mother (sounding out the first line: Sahspno!
Natasha (thoughtful and satisfied): I did it.

little skill to write them. Or the child with poor motor co-ordination may find the writing task itself rather exacting. A teacher can reduce frustration by acting as the child's scribe as she did when he first wanted his messages written down. The written text is then partly his and partly hers but the message remains the child's.

Before the end of his first year in school the child who is making good progress develops a power to read which outreaches his capacity to write. *For a preliminary period creative writing activities appear to be an important complement to a reading programme.* In the child's early contact with written language, writing behaviours seem to play the role of organizers of reading behaviours. Writing is not the only means of expressing ideas in written language (for one could use word or sentence building kits) but it does appear to help the child to come to grips with learning to attend to the significant details of written language.

Let me illustrate the problems that the very young reader has in locating what he should be attending to.

Suppose a teacher has placed an attractive picture on the wall and has asked her children for a story which she will record under it. They offer the text 'Mother is cooking' which the teacher alters slightly to introduce some features she wishes to teach. She writes,

Mother said,
'I am baking.'

If she says, 'Now look at our *story* ,' 30 percent of a new entrant group will attend to the *picture.*

If she says, 'Look at the *words* and find some you know,' between 50 and 90 percent will be searching for *letters.* If she says, 'Can you see Mother?' most will agree that they can but some *see* her in the picture, some can locate 'M' and others will locate the word 'Mother'.

Perhaps the children read in unison 'Mother is...' and the

teacher tries to sort this out. Pointing to *said* she asks, 'Does this say *is*?' Half agree it does because it has 's' in it. *'What letter does it start with?'* Now the teacher is really in trouble. She assumes that children *know* that a word is built out of letters but 50 percent of children still confuse the verbal labels 'word' and 'letter' after six months of instruction. She also assumes that the children know that the left-hand letter following a space is the 'start' of a word. Often they do not. She says, 'Look at the *first* letter. It says s-s-s-s' and her pupils make s-noises. But Johnny who knows only 'Mother' and 'I' scans the text haphazardly for something relevant, sights the *comma* and makes s-noises!

Mother said,
'I am baking.'

Teacher continues, 'What do you think Mother said? *Look at the next word* and tell me what it says.' That should be easy because most children learn 'I' early, but for a child who does not know the difference between a letter and a word 'the next word' will often be the second letter in 'said'. For other children who have not established left to right movement with return sweep the next word may be 'gnikab' because they are returning right to left along the second line. Still others may be conscientiously striving to decode the commas or the inverted commas, before they get to 'I'.

The lesson continues and the class makes a final unison statement 'Mother said, "I am cooking".' Many have focussed on the quaint letter 'k' in the middle. The teacher says, 'Does it say cooking? Look carefully. Look at the beginning. Tell me what the first letter says.' Many children may not locate the first letter. 'Does it say c-c-c-c?' Children with an intuitive awareness of the phonic identity of 'k' agree heartily. The teacher has now reached the new information for which her lesson was designed. 'It says b-b-b-b-for baking.' Some of the class are surprised to find that the 'k' they are focussing says 'b' and others gain the impression that 'baking' says 'b'.

An earnest child may be found reading the story to himself later in the day. Matching the number of word impulses he says, to the number of word patterns he sees we might hear him *read* 'Mother is cooking some cakes,' and he could be very satisfied with his effort.

One could protest that if a good teacher was aware of such difficulties and was carefully pointing to letters and words as she spoke much of the confusion would be eliminated. But that assumes rather too much of group instruction where the young child's attention does fluctuate. If the teacher examines the things she says to her class, to small groups and to individual children she may find that she takes for granted insights which some children do not have. It was discovered that learning these concepts takes place slowly over the first year at school (Reid, 1958; Downing, 1965; Clay, 1972). In a sample of 100 five year old school entrants 84 percent could locate the front of the book on entry to school but 36 percent thought that the picture rather than the print told the story. Only 27 percent failed to detect an inverted picture but 97 percent failed to detect the inversion of print in a caption book. Between 41 and 48 percent could already perform within the directional constraints required for reading behaviour and this rose to 92 percent by the end of the year. But what problems the other 8 percent faced!

Creative writing activities can be an excellent complement to a reading programme. They may be used both as a guide to the child's sophistication with the concepts of written language and as a means of directing his attention to important details in written language.

Individual Differences

The wide range of individual differences which the teacher of New Entrants can observe can be appreciated by studying some examples of children's efforts to write. Most examples of work in this book have been taken from classrooms where children learned to write with a minimum of instruction in letter formation.

When Peter first came to school he made an interesting drawing of the three bears. His attempt to print was limited to four vertical lines. The teacher wrote a simple sentence 'I like Peter's bears' and read it to him, making the point that print, like drawings, conveys messages.

I like Peter's bears!

Peter, aged 5:0

What response does Jim make to written language? His drawing of black horizontal lines crossed by a red vertical line suggests a more limited development of drawing skill. He called it a ladder and the teacher labelled it. Jim's only writing response to this recorded message was to draw a line under it.

Gary's drawing is also primitive. When he called it a fish his teacher invited him to tell her more about the picture because she was aware that Gary's oral language was well developed. Gary extended his statement and his teacher recorded 'The fish in the water.'

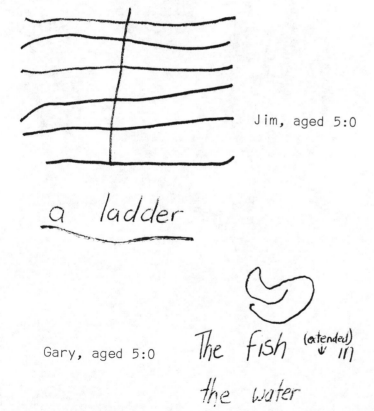

Jim, aged 5:0

a ladder

Gary, aged 5:0

The fish (extended) ↓ in

the water

It's a worm
Itsa worm

Corina, aged 5:0

Corina drew an interesting picture on her second day at school and she invented some writing at the top of the page. She told the teacher 'It's a worm' and she copied the teacher's record of the message, forming letters, words and spaces like a veteran of six months' schooling.

The children responded differently. Peter drew a complete picture but did not write, and Gary did the same. Corina drew a picture, invented writing, talked well, and copied very well. Thus, when children enter school there are large differences between them in their abilities to work with language.

Can there be Age Norms?

The examples of writing behaviour in this book were made by children who were between 4:10 and 7:0 but the ages on the samples are intended to do no more than illustrate the variability found among children. In no sense are these ages intended to represent norms because what one child discovers about print at 4:11 another equally intelligent child may not learn until 6:0. Such differences could be related to general intelligence but they could equally well occur because the experiences of the children have been different or because they have chosen to devote their attention to different aspects of their environment. I doubt whether there is a fixed sequence of learning through which all children must pass and this raises further doubts in my mind about the value of any sequenced programme for reading or writing which proceeds from an adult's logical analysis of the task and not from an observation of what children are doing, and the points at which they, the children, are becoming confused. The insights the child must gain relate to *arbitrary* conventions by which our speech is recorded and it is possible to imagine that the learning of those conventions may be approached from a variety of directions. Eventually as each convention is mastered the children acquire a common fund of concepts but the point of entry and the path of progress may be different for any two children. Chance experiences may produce new insights at any time which alter the entire learned pattern.

Questions of Method

From the child's first attempt to copy a caption to his error-free composition about an interesting event, what are the teacher's aims in creative writing? If the main aim is to help the child express his ideas effectively in print, several questions about instruction can arise.

- What is the value of copying?
- Should the teacher correct the grammatically incorrect sentence that a child dictates?
- Why do children produce error-free products after one month only to write many errors in their *later* attempts?
- Does the process simply unfold in a stimulating classroom?
- Is there an ideal sequence of skills to be developed?

It is the aim of this book to help teachers develop skills of observation and analysis that lead towards a better understanding of the acquisition process so that they will be able to decide the answers to these questions of method, according to their individual teaching strengths and the individual differences of their pupils.

Some Teaching Points

In a developmental period or during reading activities the New Entrant is often invited to draw something that interests him and to show his drawing to the teacher. She may then ask him to tell her about it. In the example Grant drew a house. When he gave the teacher the label 'house' she recorded 'A house' below his drawing in italic script. The teacher acted as the child's scribe. What did Grant attempt to write? Where did his three mock letters which are quite unlike the teacher's model come from?

The amount of text that is written for the child varies according to the teacher's aims for that particular child at that particular time. Since Grant cannot form letters yet *a very simple text* is appropriate.

Grant, aged 5:1

What were the teacher's aims for this child on this day? Were they appropriate? If so why? If not, why?

Joseph, aged 5:6

The man is gone to school.

Joseph was a Samoan boy with very little English. His teacher wrote down exactly what he said. Perhaps she wanted him to continue talking to her and not to feel criticised or corrected. Perhaps she thought that when he re-read the text he would more readily reproduce the words that were written. Readers will probably differ in their reaction to this recording of 'ungrammatical English' but is the teaching point for this child English grammar? or willingness to respond in English? or re-reading what is written? Although Joseph tried to copy the text the printing task defeated him.

For Stephen the approach was different. His teacher ruled up his book and printed 'Here is Stephen' in the lower half. He was expected to translate this message into a drawing. Why do you think he turned his book around to draw the picture and back again for the printing? Was it because he was unaware that the orientation of print and picture should be the same? Stephen wrote by *tracing over* the teacher's model. He also traced the words 'A car' which were heavily written on another page and had shown through. He seemed unaware of the mirror reversal.

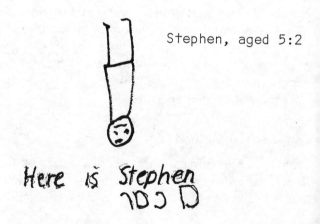

Stephen, aged 5:2

Here is Stephen

Frank is not gaining very much from copying his long statement but his teacher's aim was to preserve his willingness to produce an extended statement, a sentence of good construction, so she wrote it all down. Frank *traced over* her copy, a first step, but then attempted the more difficult task of *copying underneath the model.*

I am brushing my feeth before I go to school.

Frank, aged 5:3

Yvonne had been at school six weeks when she produced her example. She was a Samoan girl with some language problems but her visual discrimination of letter forms was quite advanced. Firstly she produced a short version of her name (Yvoe) and followed this with two good copies. Her copy of the sentence was disciplined, with spacing, capitals and punctuation and she had contrasted capital and lower case letters in 'TRAFFIC'. She seemed ready to take the next step forward, to *write down her own ideas without a copy.* It is interesting to note the flexibility of children at this stage. When Yvonne's paper was folded the teacher's ink showed through from the other side of the paper presenting her with a 'shadow' inversion of the words. Yvonne copied the inverted print wth the same control and quality as her own print in normal orientation!

Yvonne, aged 5:1

What can this five year old do?

aged 5:0

Although Amanda was just five years of age she was trying to write her own story. She managed to write *the sentence starter 'Here...'* and was praised lavishly by her teacher who finished the sentence for her. When written vocabulary is limited the child must force what he wants to say into the mould of what he is able to write. For Amanda 'Here is...' will probably remain a standard sentence for some weeks at least.

Vivianne can manage two sentences and her teacher, reading it with her, *draws her attention to two points,* an omission from the end of 'Monday', and the missing word, 'at'.

Vivianne, aged 5:3

This next example shows marked changes from the performance of five year olds. Describe what Lester's teacher might want to make him aware of now about the conventions of written language.

Lester is much older, nearly seven years, and the ideas he records are more complex. He still has many problems with written English, with letter forms (for example 'a Lot', 'and They', 'five' or 'fire'), with letter order (fluel), with word agreements (a satellites), with word forms ('went' for 'when'), and with punctuation (no full-stops in four sentences). The teacher must spend a little time and effort to work out what Lester is trying to say before she makes her comments and suggestions.

All about Rockets
They have a lot
and air and They
have a Lot of
fluel They
have instruments
and They have a
payload in the
nose cone They have
a satellites went
the stages of
off the Rockets
The fuel and
air go to
five

Lester, aged 7:0

Would this be a suitable standard of work to expect of a six year old who had been at school one year?

Tania
On   Sunday   Daddy took
us   up to   see   Jeanette.
When we   got   up   there it was
Peter's   party   and   he is three
now.   On   Saturday Cindy came
down   to   my   place and we playe-
d   underneathe   the   house. After
we   had played   under neth the hou

Tania, aged 6:0

Tania had just turned six but she controlled the conventions of written language very well. She told her story clearly with a flexible use of sentence structures and a disciplined use of capitals and punctuation, even to the possessive apostrophe. To be ready to learn the spelling of the last syllable of 'underneath' and the place of the hyphen in end-of-line breaks after one year of instruction in school is very rapid progress.

These examples indicate that teachers are helping children of similar ages who are at very different stages of awareness about written language. They must learn

- to understand that print talks
- to form letters
- to build up memories of common words they can construct out of letters

- to use those words to write messages
- to increase the number and range of sentences used
- to become flexible in the use of sentences
- to discipline the expression of ideas within the spelling and punctuation conventions of English.

The complexity of the task did not matter for Corina, Yvonne and Tania who quickly mastered the intricacies, but for those children who become stranded at some learning hurdle it is most important that their teachers are observing their progress sensitively.

The Value and Place of Copying

A poor observer of young children might assume that writing is easy to teach. All that is required is a series of models for the child to copy or trace. In time many repetitions should implant images of letters or words in his mind. Let us examine the value and limitations of these assumptions.

Anthony is five and does not know how to use a copy. But he does know how to construct a capital 'A' for his own name and it *isn't* the form used in the teacher's model. Probably the teacher's copy inspired Anthony to try his hand at writing letters, and that is a beginning. But Anthony is unable to copy until he has learnt more about print.

Tracing is the next step towards writing but with a product like this a teacher could not assume that it was traced in sequence from left to right across the line. Why should it have been? This is one problem with copying — it may not consolidate correct directional habits.

Anthony

Roger's particular method of tracing was not quite what his teacher intended and possibly had very little learning value. But he did construct and discriminate eight different forms for himself, five with letter identity (O,T,H,M,I) and two which are almost letters (K and E) and these probably had greater learning value than the copied text above them. Why?

We saw Father Christmas
| ☰ M E K H T+)

Roger, aged 5:3

Roger is beginning to discriminate between letters, placing them in separate categories, and is attending to their features in such detail that he can organize his own behaviour to begin, arrange and complete their distinctive shapes. He has learned to organize himself in two-dimensional space.

When the child gains confidence in tracing letters he spontaneously tries his hand at copying underneath. There is a large discrepancy between Roberta's controlled tracing and her disjointed 'copying', but it would be wrong to assume that she should continue tracing. Roberta's work shows clearly that she needs to gain more control over copying, so that she can deal with spaces and shapes in a more controlled way.

a rocket going to splash
o 'OCRt ɔɔɔ + ʃplpʃ'

Roberta

However, when a writing programme depends, day after day, on repetitious copying a child's attempts may readily show deterioration rather than improvement as the example shows. Perhaps fatigue or disinterest are responsible, or perhaps the child is copying his own previous attempt each time.

Breakfast is here
Brektfat is nee
Brckℇt is no
Breeft is no
Br ft k no

Even self-scheduled copying sessions produce results which are not exciting compared with creative attempts. Copying helps the child to form his first few letters or words but it is rather a slow and laborious way to extend one's repertoire. Is there any other method?

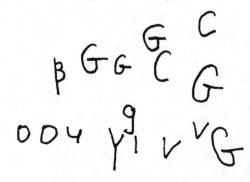

Michael, aged 5:9

Plans of Action

There are several research reports which suggest that children of five years learn faster if they are able to organize for themselves a sequence of movements than they do if their hands are passively moved through that sequence. If the child is able to teach himself the movements he requires to make one or two letter forms, this also seems to teach the child *how to organize* his approach to new forms. When he develops some internal procedure for making an 'S' or an 'M' he may make new letters by modifying these first patterns of movements and so manage to write g and 'H'.

Letters which are very distinctive present little problem. However letters which are similar may not be identified by

the child as different and he may treat as the same three different letters (h,n,r,) because they all have 'tunnels'. When a wrong letter form is produced consistently the child is using one movement pattern for two forms and is overlooking the critical feature that establishes the difference between two letters (h,n; e,a or d; b seen as 'φ'). He can be confronted with the contrast before the habit of letter formations becomes too firmly established.

the ship is or the ocean

Examples of such confusions occur in the next sample. Trying to copy "A whale with his nose cut off" Joan writes

hɔs cut off
nose cut off

This child groups 'h' and 'n', 'ɔ' and 'o', 'e' and 'c' and ' ʜ ' and 'ff' as the same, which they are *in some respects*. If a teaching situation confronts the child with the new contrast he may learn it as a flash of insight and he may not need tedious repetitive copying to establish the new letter identity. However a wise teacher would not attempt to develop all the above distinctions at once, but would establish one firmly over several lessons before asking the child to attend to the next teaching point.

2. Questions of Development and Learning

Gross Approximations

The average child who enters school may write his name in part or in full but this is about the limit of his constructive skill in written language. Some children know much more than this and others have not progressed beyond the circles and random forms of early drawing. Piaget has described a sequential change over the years 2:6 to 7:0 in children's ability to copy forms but the variability found among children of any age in the ability to copy specific forms is wide.

Out of a primitive drawing skill emerges a letter such as 'O', a form found in the scribble of two to three year olds. When 'O' is joined roughly this may produce an overshoot, $\wp$, an undershoot, $\cup$, and a spiralling effect. ς

Accidental discoveries like these might bring a child close to new letters like $\eth$ (d or a or e), forms like $\subset$ (c), and forms like ς (b or 6). Careful recording of children's writing would be unlikely to reveal any set sequence of letter discovery because individual experiences differ greatly, but the child's early attempts at drawing and scribbling develop into later writing behaviour.

It is useful to think of the two printed English alphabets, capital and lower case, as 52 geometric forms to which must be added an extra 'ɑ' and 'ɡ'. About 11 letters are perceived by most children as similar in upper and lower case — c,k,p,s,u,v,w,x,y,z, — (Clay, 1966) but this leaves 43 shapes to be distinguished and identified, a task which must take time to learn. An adult trying to learn the Russian alphabets in print and script would have a comparable task except that the adult would already appreciate the alphabetic principle, whereas the average school entrant has yet to master this concept. Letter knowledge seems to expand outwards from a particular knowledge of a few letters.

Two features of the learning process warrant some special emphasis. The first things learnt will be *gross approximations* which later become refined: weird letter forms, invented words, make-believe sentences. Such creative efforts suggest that the child is reaching out towards the principles of written language and any instruction should encourage him to continue to do this. However, as individual letters and words become recognizable the adult must realise that this knowledge is very *specific*. 'Ian' rejects that spelling of his name, claiming that HIS name is written 'IAN'. Jenny has developed the habit of writing her name as 'Jehhy' and refuses to acknowledge the correct spelling as her own name. Because early learning is *both approximate and specific* any one new insight may change the child's perception of the entire system drastically, or may even disorganize it. This seems to be because, at first, there is so little system and so much that is new.

The characteristics of gross approximation and specificity demand that the teacher of school entrants *knows an individual child's progress* to date. She must keep samples of work arranged chronologically and must work hard at understanding what the child is trying to say in his written expression. Adults seem to be reluctant to bother with a jumbled set of letters in early writing or a story that has been written from right to left. They prefer not to read what the child is saying until he presents it in an easily read form. Those who make the effort will find a rich commentary on each child's earliest learning about print encapsulated in his accumulated attempts to write.

Flexible Control of the Writing System

Errors which mean Progress

In speech a sentence is produced or generated within a matter of seconds and there is little delay between the beginning and the end. Yet, even in adult conversation the grammatical structure of the early part of a sentence is sometimes not the one with which the speaker finishes. When a young child attempts to write a story the mechanical aspects of the task create a very long delay between the first letter and the last full stop. In the tedious labour of formulating new words in print the child often loses the meaning or the grammatical structure he began with. This is more likely with ambitious efforts than it is with short simple sentences. One child had three attempts at a short sentence without full success.

Trial 1	the man is picki	(crossed out)
Trial 2	the man is picking dig big apples	(turned to a clean page)
Trial 3	the man is picking a big apples	

The task of retelling a story in sequence is even more difficult. The account of 'El Torito' falls short of literary merit

the man is picking a big apples

Peter, aged 5:10

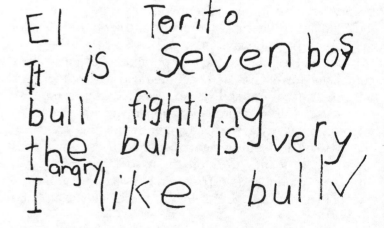

El Torito
It is seven bo$
bull fighting
the bull is very
angry
I like bull √

but it is a delightful attempt at a book precis by a very small boy.

One of the problems is created by the delay needed to carry out the motor movements required for a long statement so that the verb tenses fail to agree (as the next example shows). Or the child who is creative with language

The dinghy is gone down   the river

and it   has not sunk   and it   went to far

and it went to The right Side

Katie, aged 5:5

might involve himself in complex grammatical structures, which he cannot quite discipline in writing.

The boy who
had some
wings to fly
like the
birds. But he
went higher than
the birds and
bees. he went
hads high hads
a aeroplane
or higher.

The little
boy who
ate vegetables
he ate fruit.
he ate corn
he drak his milk
and he drak his
soup. and befor
he was thin befor

Another source of error is the child's current knowledge of grammar in spoken English. By five years the average child has made considerable progress with the basic sen-

tence patterns of the language but he still has many details of syntax to learn. In the last example the words 'hads high hads' suggest that this structure is only partly understood by the child.

This problem of limitations in the child's grammatical competence causing errors in his written work is even more apparent when the child's language development is retarded. If he cannot generate complex English sentences in his speech he cannot be expected to do this easily in writing. Children for whom English is a second language, or for whom standard English is a new dialect, have problems of this kind as the following examples suggest. They may have been written down as the child would speak.

I came to
the flower
show. If my
father gaves me
a ride.

In this case copying may be used to advantage, to familiarise a child with a grammatical structure which he does not use, or does not use correctly or does not use fluently. Research suggests that teaching points of this kind are clear to the child if only one new feature of correction is made. What would a teacher correct in this example?

the   people is has them
birthay

Perhaps she would say
The people *are having* a birthday

What should she correct in this story?

> When Henry
> grows up
> he well be
> a lollipop man
> and sold
> lollipops to
> all the
> people.
> So now he
> solds lollipops.

Consider the following 'red pencil' attempts to improve syntax. The child wrote his story and the teacher wrote over it in blue ink as underlined:

I maked a	I <u>made</u> a
TenT. my littel	<u>tent</u>, <u>with</u> my <u>little</u>
SiSter is three	<u>sister</u> <u>who</u> is three.
my brother is five.	<u>My</u> brother is five.
today is my brother.	<u>To</u>day is my brother's
birthday.	birthday.

I wonder whether the child ever really looked at the altered text. He probably learned none of the nine teaching points the teacher tried to make which was six or seven too many.

There will always be errors in word detail if the child is motivated to express his ideas, rather than merely stay within the confines of the vocabulary with which he is familiar and the skills he can control.

Sometimes the error is a slip in letter formation.

Sometimes it is a copying error, involving sequence of letters

This is a tree and in Atumn the leaves foll off this tree and turn different Colours.

When a child asks for a word teachers should take care to supply the one that is needed. This girl was able to detect the error and tried to erase it.

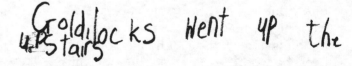

In the next sample the use of 'me' deserves attention. Before one assumes that the child speaks with this grammatical error 'me surf board' one could weigh the possibility that this is an error of letter-sound relationship, and that this child possibly thinks that when he writes 'me' he is actually writing 'my'. I would want to hear him read his story before I could be sure.

when I was at the beach

I splash some water over me Father and He laughed and then I went on me surf board but I couldnt surf So I got way out and then I sit on the surf and I went fast and I board figgy and I was he and I played caught Bill and then I went home.

Observation of children suggests that they do not learn about language on any one level of organization *before* they manipulate units at higher levels. (Many teaching schemes imply that this is so.) When they know a few letters they can produce several words, and with several words they can make a variety of sentences. A mere 52 letters would generate all the contents of a massive dictionary and some eight basic sentence patterns could describe all the grosser structures of English prose. As the child learns to write there is a rich intermingling of language learning *across* levels which probably accounts in some way for the fast progress which the best children can make. A simplification achieved by dealing firstly with letters, then with words, and finally with word groups may be easy for teachers to understand but children learn on all levels at once.

In the sections which follow, what the child learns about letters, words and word groups is described separately merely because I find it easier to report it that way. The individual child's progress in mastering the complexity of the writing system seems to involve letters, words, and word groups all at the one time, at first in approximate, specific and what seem to be primitive ways and later with considerable skill. If there is an acquisition sequence which can be described for all children I have not been able to discover it in these examples and so I am forced to report the changes in separate sections with all the risks of misinterpretation which that implies.

3. Concepts and Principles

THE RECURRING PRINCIPLE

In Drawing

The effect of a string of terrace houses was achieved by this child in a community where terrace houses hardly exist. It is a good example of repetition or the recurring principle.

Terence, aged 5:9

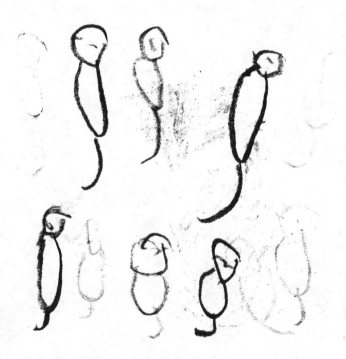

The same principle can be found in the drawings of a human figure which some children produce at this age. On several different occasions, spaced well apart in time, a child may produce very similar drawings which suggest a schema or programme of movements for producing 'a man' or 'a lady'.

20

Some are very primitive attempts, but others are elaborately designed with a recurrent basic form.

Nicola, aged 5:4

In Writing

A child who knows only a few letters or words can take a short cut to a long statement by repeating the same symbol again and again and again. This trick of constructing long messages by writing strings of letters also may give practice which leads to habitual responses, executed smoothly and swiftly. When the copying task is set by the teacher it might be a boring activity, which can lead to serious deterioration of effort to make good letter forms as the example illustrates.

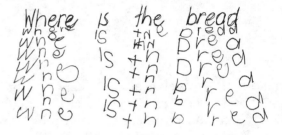

Yet as a self-initiated process repetition can provide a wonderful sense of accomplishment.

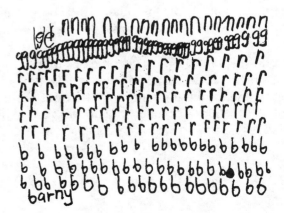

Words, like letters can be treated according to the recurring principle. Repeating a word one has mastered produces a long statement of which one must be proud.

It is interesting to observe at what stage repetition of words begins and when it ends. Why does the child spontaneously repeat certain forms, (the recurring principle), and why does he begin to vary the forms (the flexibility principle)? Written language does not permit one to vary the forms very much without changing the whole meaning, so that a slight variation of 'Look' to 'Loor', in the next example, is not 'successful' flexibility. On the other hand the variation of 'This' to 'THIS' would be a permissible one in written English.

The recurring principle must become disciplined by some constraints on what can recur in English. When he is older the pupil will learn the limitation that two but never three consecutive repetitions of letters are allowable and only in rare instances can three words be repeated in English.

Sherryl Lyn, aged 5:6

Terence, aged 5:7

THE DIRECTIONAL PRINCIPLES

Signs, Letters and Single Words

Language is written in two-dimensional space according to a set of conventions which the adult reader takes for granted. Observation records of early reading behaviour showed that when children were asked to 'Read it with your finger' they moved from left to right ($\rightarrow$), right to left ($\leftarrow$), top to bottom and bottom to top, snaked back and forth over the lines ($\gtrless$), and even tried left to right pointing to words while progressing right to left over the lines! The problem was solved by one child who used the centre of the reading book as a focus and proceeded right to left on a left page and left to right on a right page $\boxed{\leftarrow | \rightarrow}$ This behaviour fluctuates during the first year of instruction emphasizing the children's uncertainty. There is an increasing dominance of the appropriate directional movements but some children arrive at a personal consistency which is wrong for reading or writing English. A consistent right to left visual survey of the short lines of beginning reading books may not be detected by the busy teacher, but it becomes obvious whether the child has directional problems when he is asked to read 'with his finger'.

For correct directional behaviour a top-left starting position is mandatory, movement must proceed from left to right, and a return sweep is taken back to a left hand position under the starting point, to establish the top to bottom progression. A pattern of movements is required, carried out in a particular sequence. The directional learning to be mastered by the new entrant can be described as a four step schema made up of the following stages:

1. Start top left.
2. Move left to right across the word or line.
3. Return down left.
4. Locate next starting point.

When a child produces a single line of print he has already begun to appreciate *part* of the directional pattern. He lists his letters from left to right from an appropriate starting position. On the next two examples these first two stages are supplemented by the downward movement, but not the return sweep. The first example is copying behaviour, and the second is the child's own effort.

Sherryl Lyn, aged 5:4, wrote a letter to Nana.

Jenny, aged 5:6, wrote music. This sample of writing was the 312th collected since her fifth birthday.

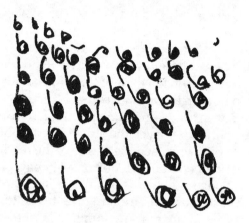

Full understanding of the four aspects of the directional pattern was evident in the next example. The child understood that speech could be written down in symbols starting at the top left, moving from left to right, returning down left and repeating the pattern. She was being consistent when she attempted to write 'music' according to the directional principles of written language. How was she to know that we choose a different set of arbitrary conventions for writing down music? Music does retain the left to right and return down left convention, but there are other features built into that code.

Lists of words, one under the other, demonstrate good control over the directional principles of written English. The elements in the sequences are letters strung out across a horizontal line but the children retain the directional pattern 'Start top left, move left to right, and return down left' in all its spatial characteristics.

At an earlier stage of development the child might have peppered the individual letters randomly around his page, producing all the elements of the known word, but not disciplined according to the directional principles required in writing English. For example, it is unwise to assume that the relationship of letters put together from left to right to make words, is obvious to children. Ian seemed to know the elements in his signature but does not yet recognise the principle of invariant letter sequence in words.

A false starting position is an important source of deviation from the pattern of directional principles. When a child

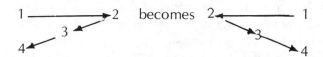

The child starts at the top right, moves right to left and returns down right. At the same time the letters are often reversed so that they *retain* the spatial relationships in the linear sequence. Well-established habits of writing some letter forms (see the letter 'e' below) seem to act like a brake to prevent the whole movement schema going into reverse.

Peter, aged 5:4

Such variation may be accidental or it may be a more deliberate testing of limits but it often follows some time after some correct directional principles have been observed in an individual child's writing.

If such behaviour is observed *the starting position* appears to be critical for appropriate responding. The young child trying to locate himself on a page of paper may choose any starting point. If he happens to choose the top left it is difficult to move in the wrong direction. If he chooses left and right alternately on many occasions he may *confuse himself* about directional behaviour and print. At this point the teacher may well introduce some suitable sign (a cross or a green sticker) to help him locate his starting place and

with some experience in writing happens to start at the top right of the page in error, the pressure of his sequencing habits seems to make him reverse the whole pattern of directional movements. This means that he not only begins in the wrong place but he also carries out most of the other directional principles *in relation to that false start.* It is as if the whole movement schema had been flipped over or reversed.

prevent a process of self-confusion from occurring. Research results suggest that the four parts of the directional pattern have been mastered by children after about six months at school and by then the sequenced behaviour is more or less under control. While some flexibility should be encouraged in early contacts with print giving children freedom to explore, invent and vary actual forms, the teacher may become more deliberate in her attempts to prevent confusions in the child after six months at school.

Changes in the letter order or orientation within individual words persist long after a correct directional pattern for lines has been established.

saw	dog	chidlen	oo	Potrice	littel
was	boy	children	zoo	Patrice	little

Errors like these result from problems with visual analysis of letter sequence from left to right, rather than an inability to establish the directional movement pattern.

Being Flexible About Direction

Children turn letters around, decorate them, and evolve new signs as they explore the limits within which a sign can vary. It would be surprising if such flexibility was limited only to letters and the following examples show the same experimental approach applied to words. At times the flexibility arises from difficulty in remembering — it is a failure to produce a correct pattern already known. But at other times children apparently engage in deliberate variation of known or observed patterns. At this early stage they are not constrained by the limits of print conventions which adults insist upon. In the example of copying from a packet of breakfast cereal, the child has kept to the model for the first two attempts. Then what happens?

He attempts a double change, — a right to left sequencing and top to bottom inversion. This could have occurred because he failed to apply the directional principle of return-down-left. But it might equally well be the result of wanting to vary the product — a curiosity to see what happened when a different approach was tried. He may have turned his paper upside down to achieve this effect. Because we cannot observe the child as he writes we do not know the reasons for this product.

The flexibility principle is sometimes applied by the child to an aspect of written language which is inflexible, such as the directional pattern. The child who produced the next example had been working with correct directional principles for two months. These reversed and inverted words could have been a conscious attempt to experiment with or vary the directional pattern.

Lyn, aged 5:2

THE GENERATING PRINCIPLE

Applied to Letters and Signs

A very easy way to extend one's statements is to know some elements and to have several plans for combining or arranging those elements. One can then produce new statements in an inventive way. A child with a repertoire of only three signs could generate a line of print like this:

When a child realises that letter elements can recur *in variable patterns* he has made a great deal of progress. Although a teacher might be delighted with a careful attempt to copy some print she has written she might well be more delighted with the following samples, because in each case the child has understood the principle that long statements are generated from a limited number of symbols.

In the next example Alex (with a signature of Xℓ1A) has communicated a message in his picture and he has generated a long statement (string of signs) underneath. On the back of this work sample the teacher wrote her note of regret.

'He was supposed to copy
"We went to the library"
from the blackboard.'

That was the task she set her group or class. It may well be that Alex may have learned more from his attempt to produce a string of letters than from copying a message he could not read. If, on the other hand, Alex had shown no change in this behaviour for several weeks and appeared to be settling into a habit with which he was too content, then she had cause for regret. But if this were true the teacher's solution of providing a copying task was not the only one possible and perhaps not the best one.

The next example warrants close attention because it illustrates a number of things that this child, like Alex, had understood. What did she understand about

signs?
the flexibility principle?
the recurring principle?
the directional principle?
the generating principle?

few letter forms can discover this principle. One little girl wrote down the names of all her dolls, so she thought. She used the few signs she knew and a few copied letters to construct word-like strings and staunchly maintained that these recorded the dolls' actual names.

It seems that she already had some rules for word-making. She might almost have said to herself,

Jenny, aged 5:4

This example shows considerable control over some of the unwritten rules required in writing English. The ability to construct many words out of 26 letters, and many sentences out of a limited vocabulary, becomes of very great importance in sentence and story writing. This will be referred to as the generating principle.

Applied to words

The generating principle can be applied to words. When the child discovers that words are built up out of signs he can invent words from signs he knows. The child who knows a

You use the signs you know (the sign concept, J o i). You copy others from books (the copying principle, source of A, U, D, N).
You use the same signs twice (the recurring principle, oo, uu) and you turn old signs upside down or around (the flexibility principle N2).
That makes a new pattern for a different doll, (the generating principle). Now you say what you have written (the letter-sound principle).

Tonn,4i

'This says Sleepy-eye Doll.'

AUUDO

'This says Katrina.'

Jooi2

'This says Debbie.'

This child was 4:11 and had not yet begun school or learned to read. How useful were her discoveries?

For another child the boundary between drawing and word symbols is less clear. Is this a drawing, an invention, or an approximation to a word?

The next child has constructed an example out of known signs, and seems to appreciate that some letters occur together twice (but never three times) in English, and added a figure 8 to increase the variety of symbols.

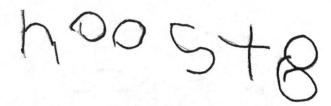

This reminds me of young children whose efforts to say the alphabet run a b c d e f g k o p 6 8 fiveteen.

Although ACE looks familiar, and suggests a sophisticated knowledge of playing cards or aviation, in all probability the child invented the word. That you might discover it to be a real word would probably not surprise the child of four or five because that is what she supposed would happen if she 'wrote words'. The adult reader is expected to know the message.

The generating principle can be used to fill a gap when memory for detail fails. The little girl who wrote 'boats' at school one day, had forgotten some of its features by the time she reported this to her mother but made up the missing parts and produced 'toos'.

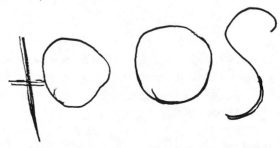

Steven, aged about 5:6

In the search for the rules of the code one little boy thought he had solved its mysteries. 'If you end with what you start with this may be the cue to the whole pattern.' His rule was inadequate for generating 'Mother' and 'Father' but the initial letters, the correct number of letters and the concept of generating words from letters according to rules are useful concepts. He has probably made progress.

The generating principle becomes very important in sentence-making which is discussed later in Chapter 6.

Steven used the generating principle applied to letters to extend his statement when his writing vocabulary was limited to the one word 'The'.

Catherine

Catherine found her name too long to remember in detail but with a knowledge of some detail, a vague notion of length and the aid of the generating principle, she produced a name to her satisfaction.

THE INVENTORY PRINCIPLE

Letters

Until I observed five year olds closely I had no idea that they took stock of their own learning systematically. Their work sometimes shows how spontaneously they arrange or order the things they have learned into inventories. In the next example the child has made an exhaustive list of all the letters he 'knows', that is all those for which he has some mental plan and for which he does not need a copy. This same approach will be seen later in word lists and in sentence lists. The activity undoubtedly has some value for the child in systematising those items which he can recall and which have become part of *his* written repertoire. But such an inventory can also tell the teacher a great deal. It records those fluent responses which the particular child has 'at his finger-tips', and it suggests the unfilled gaps.

The next inventory is limited in number of units but like many lists constructed by children the separate identity of the units seems to have been emphasized.

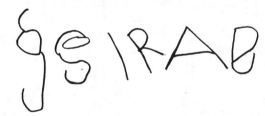

Yet another way of documenting the separate identity of individual letters is to make a set of letter cards. In the examples shown this was a self-scheduled activity.

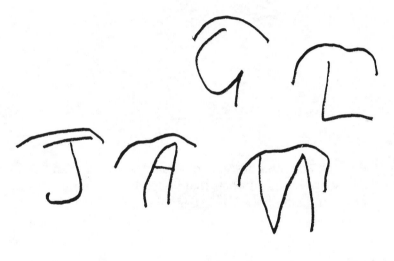

One type of structure is to group all the members of a set, such as the alphabet.

Another type of structure is to match symbols which are equivalent in the code, such as capital and lower case forms, or to pair a letter with a word which uses it initially.

Aa   Bb

Cc   Dd

Ee   Ff

Gg   Hh

Ii

When such activities are self-scheduled, at home or in free time in school, one suspects that the child is exploring the structure of the alphabet code even though the set of symbols is copied.

Words

The stock-taking activity noted at the level of signs or letters can also be seen when the child knows a few words. He seems to like to list them in exhaustive lists which explore all the words he can produce without copies, as if he were saying. 'These are all the words I can write.' Sometimes these inventories are copied lists; at other times they are an attempt to list all members of a limited set — family, friends, words beginning with a particular letter, words ending similarly and so on.

Two further examples of inventories are included to show the work of two different children which is remarkably similar. The vocabulary is not very different, the span or size of the produced vocabulary is four and five words, the letter formation and sequencing problems seem to be similar and both children make a false start and recover their directional principles later.

S
She
See
SKxd
Sqid
So
Sad
Shaki
Short
Stop

O
Oh
ane
on
On
of
off
onee

TAGKTANKTAX
TENNISTERRIER
THEATRE
THERMOMETRE
TIETIGER

KOOB
Tohh
See
Tehhy
look

Towards the end of the first year the mere listing of words is no longer favoured by the children making better progress. Sometimes their lists (invented, created or copied) show a search for order or structure, as this primitive and early sample suggests.

Another type of structure is to match symbols which are equivalent in the code, such as capital and lower case forms, or to pair a letter with a word which uses it initially.

Jenny, aged 5:3

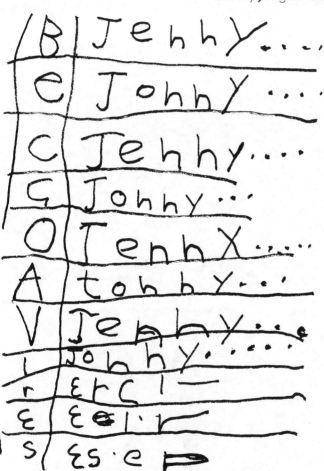

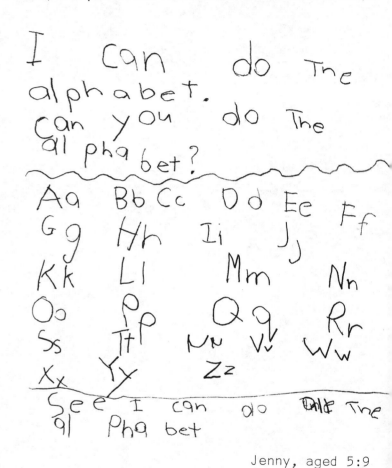

Jenny, aged 5:9

Numbers are another type of symbol which can be listed like these samples of Arabic and Roman numerals produced by children of this age.

Yet another was 32 titles of children's records played on several weekly radio sessions.

An interesting contrast is found in two lists from one little girl taken about two months apart. In the first she wrote 'all the words I know' which amounted to 65. (Only a partial list is shown.) This might be called an inclusive list of writing vocabulary. In the second she listed all the words in a book which she did not know, that is, an exclusive list of reading vocabulary. It was her own idea to carry out this activity in her play time at home.

Kay, aged 5:2

A list of stories included in the contents of a book was another type of inventory found.

Kay, aged 5:4

THE CONTRASTIVE PRINCIPLE

Letters

It is a feature of man's thinking, reflected in his language, that ideas can be contrasted with opposite ideas. Sometimes the urge to see all things in black and white is a handicap to clear thinking, but it is a special kind of structuring to establish opposites. Another form of contrast occurs when two things that are at the same time similar and different are compared. Some samples of children's unprompted exploration of print and shapes, showed them apparently applying this principle. Early letters made with lines and angles contrast one with another, in some feature, (A, H, M, W).

The next example is a perceptual contrast where the child made up a list of items and asked 'Are they the same?' Some items are intended to be the same. Others are contrasted, in some way, but usually that way is by presenting a mirror image. The other two examples are of semantic contrast.

As a final example let us take a boy's letter-play before he went to sleep at night. This five year old had a sheet of squared paper which structured his activity. It is possible to see three inventories in this record but what are the contrasts being explored in the word list? The most obvious is the contrast of capital and lower case forms which occurs throughout. But reading down the list what prompts the change to another word? Rhyme? Letter-sound relationships? Size of word? Meaning? He ended the page with his signature, carefully recording this in two contrasted forms. Presumably he then went to sleep content with his achievement.

It was a surprise to me to find children creating contrasts in visual form, letters, meaning, and sounds. The examples come only from some of the children who made rapid progress in learning to read, but appear to be further evidence of the urge, not only to explore, but also to arrange in some order the characteristics of print. However, the practice of pairing two similar things in order to emphasize the *differences* is what we commonly do to help children make new discriminations. The contrastive principle in operation tells the teacher what dimensions of difference the child can already control.

There may be an important teaching principle in this urge to list, order and structure which has shown up in the spontaneous products of these children. There seems to be a need to take stock, a need to re-order known items, perhaps to group, and then to re-group in different ways to encourage flexibility.

```
1  S  E  4  5  d  r  8  9  0
A  B  C  D  E  F  H  I  L  K  I  M  N  O  P  Q  R  S  t  U
V  W  X  Y  S    a  n  d
                 A  N  D
                 t  n  e
                 T  H  E
                 i  s
                 I  S
                 d  o  g
                 D  O  G
                 c  a  t
                 C  A  T
                 b  o  o  K
                 B  o  o  K
                 l  o  o  k
                 L  o  o  K
                 s  e  e
                 S  E  E
                 a
                 A
                 w  e
                 w  e
                 t  o
                 T  o
                 d  a  v  i  d
                 a  A  V  I  d
```

THE ABBREVIATION PRINCIPLE

The abbreviation principle is not very significant for this age group of children because it occurs only rarely in examples of their writing, but it is interesting to record an early awareness of it in a few children's records. I am not thinking here of the child who signs his name with its first letter without knowing what the rest of the letters are. The abbreviation principle refers to the deliberate attempt to use one symbol, implying a full word, which the child could fill out or get help in filling out if he were asked to.

This figure contains instructions for colouring with a careful distinction made between 'blue' and 'black'. The last example was possibly copied, and perhaps its message could not be read out in words although the meaning of the message would probably be understood.

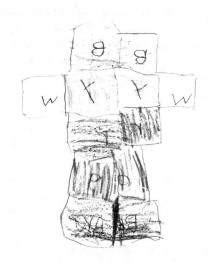

PROBLEMS OF PAGE ARRANGEMENT

A child may know the directional principles and operate within them when his page is large enough. He encounters new difficulties when he cannot fit his word or his sentence in a line or on a page. At first he adopts an easy solution and fills any left-over spaces with left-over words, ignoring at that moment any constraints of directional principles. The translation of the example is 'mouse, hedgehog, a rat and a rabbit' and it was first dictated to mother, who wrote a copy, which the child then reproduced. The directional principles are retained surprisingly well for a child who was just five years, but the last left-over word fills a gap at the left of the page.

The trouble children have with keeping to the horizontal possibly stems from immaturity in visual-motor co-ordination rather than from problems of page arrangement. The child seems to know what is required but has insufficient control to carry it out.

The question of left-overs arises: Heather ran out of line, but found a space at the left of her sentence.

This boy's attempt began too low on his page with 'Can you see. . .' so he returned to the top left hand corner to write 'the' and then split the word 'tiger' to fit the space left on the right of the page.

copying at 5:0

Terence, aged 5:8

The left-over problems of page arrangement are different from the directional problems of false starts and reversed directional schema, in that they usually occur after the directional schema has been mastered.

The next example on the left is difficult to read but the writer has not violated the directional principles or the letter sequencing principles. Her text, copied from a book cover reads 'vegetabull, story and pictures'. One the reverse side she copied the name of the author and illustrator. In the example on the right a girl has had page arrangement problems with 'Mother cooking dinner. Father mowing. See Paul and Kay.' In meeting these she has violated some of the directional principles. When this happens in the work of competent children after they have apparently mastered the directional schema it may indicate that they have encountered some new difficulty which is demanding the child's attention and distracting him from other things. This new difficulty could be page arrangement.

A most complicated example of this page arrangement trouble occurred when one little girl tried to write a book. She folded some paper and tore it to shape, producing a four page booklet. She asked her mother to write the text 'I colour my book twice a week. I draw on paper twice a week.' She took the two long sentences stretched across the paper and tried to transcribe these on to the tiny pages of her little book. She was not aware of the importance of the space between words, and had poor control over letter forms and their correct orientation. But she did know something about the sequencing of a story page by page. The most confusing aspect of the product is her willingness to break words anywhere and to put her last left-over word 'week' in any left-over space. Word breaks and page breaks are, at this time, beyond her understanding.

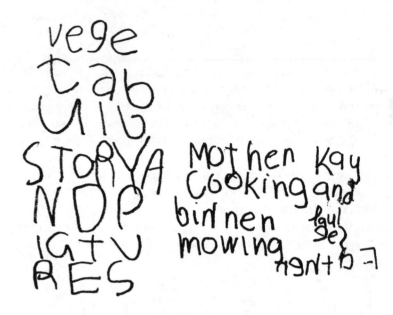

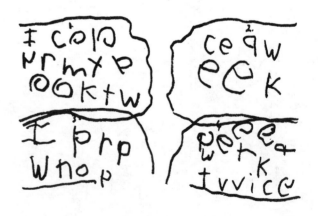

The elusive margin is another common problem of page arrangement. The arrows are one attempt by a teacher to solve this. What are others?

The   Judges
← Came   to   help
←   me   to   do
←   My   Sand
     Saucer   and
←   do   my   Jar
of   to   Flowers
←   and   My
     Floating   Bowl.

4. Signs: The Alphabet, Punctuation, and Signatures

Written English uses 52 letter signs (and two a's and g's) and my typewriter has another 11 signs for punctuation — ?',.;:''(-)! A set containing 65 members is a large amount of discrimination learning for any child, especially for one as young as five or six years.

The Flexibility Principle

From your experience of print you would probably class most of the letters in this example as 'proper' letter forms in English, but this child was probably only experimenting with forms.

TOIOH

By the same token you would probably regard some of these as non-English forms

HeꟼꟼꟼY

but the second child's level of achievement is about the same as that of the previous example. Young children produce mixtures of real letters, mock letters and innovations or inventions when their knowledge of print is still limited. With considerable flexibility they explore the limits of al-

lowable variation in the alphabetic signs. It is as if they were posing the following questions to themselves.

How far can one deviate from a form before it ceases to be that form? Or, when is a sign not a sign?

How far can one alter a known sign before one has made it into a sign of different identity? Or, when is a sign a new sign?

Are the letters below allowable variations on the letter 'd'?

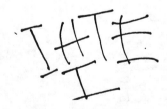

What can be done with curly letters? Are they like 'e' or 'c'? Is it possible to discover a new sign?

The flexibility principle leads to the invention of new signs when the child is aware that a wide range of signs exist, but does not know what this range is. Such flexibility probably leads to the discovery of more and more orthodox letter forms.

Left to experiment with letter forms children will create a variety of new symbols by re-positioning or decorating the standard forms. In this way they explore the limits within which each letter may vary and still retain its identity. Many 'errors' in children's early writing must be regarded as indicators of such flexibility. Can you turn a letter around? For some letters like 'e' and 's' it makes little difference to the message but for reversible letters the answer is emphatically 'No!' It is surprising how many letters change their identity if they are turned around, as the following alphabets show.

One assumes that children extend their letter repertoire by copying, but when children are left free to write they seldom copy and more often invent. One is tempted to assume that invention and flexible variation are easier than copying. The flexibility principle as it applies to copying versus creating varies from child to child and possibly with

a	b	c	d	e	f	g	h	i	j	k	l	m
b	d	c	b	e	f	g	n	i	j	k	l	m
a	q	c	q	e	f	a	p	i	i	k	w	m
p	q	c	p	e	f	g	h	i	j	k	l	w

n	o	p	q	r	s	t	u	v	w	x	y	z
n	o	q	p	r	s	t	u	v	w	x	y	z
u	o	b	d	r	s	f	n	ʌ	w	x	ʎ	z
u	o	d	b	r	s	t	n	ʌ	w	x	ʎ	z

intelligence. But presumably teachers want children eventually to create their own stories, not just to copy, and there may be some virtue in teaching in a manner which preserves this early inventiveness.

Punctuation Signs

Even in the first few months of school the child's writing may be peppered with punctuation marks. Adults may think of these as signs which *follow* the learning of letter forms but a sign is a sign for young children whether it be punctuation or alphabet. An alert child assumes that all signs are necessary and important.

Note the punctuation in these examples.

Arkadev and Braverman (1967) provide an interesting discussion on the recognition of letter forms in 'Teaching Computers to Recognise Patterns.'

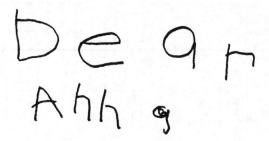

Katherine and Ian were very impressed with fullstops.

And the question mark appears in "Can you see the tiger?", a text which suffered from page arrangement problems but which is a creditable effort at copying letters, words and punctuation.

Early writing behaviour is often punctuated by elaborated dots over 'i' and 'j' which diminish in importance as the child's attention shifts from the characteristics of the forms to the meaning of the message conveyed.

Alert children who are interested in print not only notice punctuation but also gain some awareness of its meaning. While the technical labels of fullstop or inverted commas are of little value to the young child, there are places in his reading where a simple definition of punctuation in terms of function may improve the fluency of his reading.

    'It tells you when you've said enough.'

    'It asks a question.'

    'Somebody's speaking.'

    'It marks a little pause.'

These explanations offered by young children indicate an appreciation of the function of these signs in written English.

Signatures as Signs

Signatures are very personal signs. It is only a rare child that learns any other words before attempting to write some of his own name. At first the child recognises the initial letter (a capital) of his name as a sign. It occurs beside a space and it is bigger than the other letters. But at this stage the other letters are not usually noticed and their order is not of importance to the child. If the teacher makes any child's name into a three piece jig-saw puzzle at this stage he may place the pieces in any order and even upside-down!

Michael

Gradually the child's signature evolves, indicating an increasing awareness of the features that occur in print. Sherryl Lyn's signature demonstrates the grosser forms of change, during six months and Patrice's signature shows slower evolution.

petrice aged 5:0

pp+rice

pp+rice

pptrice aged 5:1

pptrice

petrice aged 5:5

petlice

peirlce

patrice aged 5:9   patrice aged 5:11

patrice

Sherrilyn

sherry Lyn

Sherryl Lyn, aged 5:5 to 6:0

Sherri Lynn
p.....

With a very shaky hand Alex uses his name to cover the page, in a style that is reminiscent of the letter drawings discussed later (p.50).

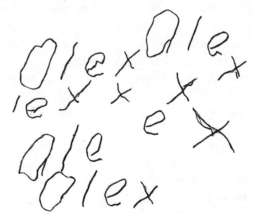

but Edward (Chinese) has a mature signature which records two names with a space between, showing an appreciation of the conventions used when writing word groups.

Edward Wang

As the child records his name the repetition of this familiar word may establish some very important concepts, namely, the invariant set of letters and order of letters that make up a remembered word.

The child has a name which was not selected by his parents for its potential contribution to his writing skill. But of any word in his mother tongue his name is likely to be the most highly motivating word to want to write. When he has mastered the initial letter (his first capital letter although he does not know this), it has the quality of a monogram — that letter equals him. To adults who understand the principle of abbreviation, the letter stands for his name, but to the child it *is* his name. Whatever the mental schema which leads to repeated productions of this one letter, he can develop this awareness in two different directions.

Firstly, little by little he adds the other letters of his name, in appropriate sequence until he can run through four or five letters. 'Ian' is more fortunate in this respect than 'Christopher' but if the latter masters the whole name he has a greater command over letters and over sequencing behaviour than the former. Presumably there is some mental programme for this behaviour because it can be repeated ad infinitum.

Secondly, he may distinguish between HIS monogram and that of some other people that interest him, his friends, pets, or family members. This line of development introduces him to other items in the set of capital letters.

A child who is beginning to discover print and who is shown an alphabet randomly arranged may correctly respond to certain letters — 'That's in my name.' He may also identify several letters as occurring in the names of his classmates or siblings; 'That's Mary,' and 'Peter' and 'Wally' and 'That's my mother'. With a few letters differentiated in this way the child is ready to form a writing vocabulary. His first efforts use the letters he knows but the more highly motivated he is to write, by creating his own word and letter forms, or by copying, the more likely he is to discover new letter forms, new word forms, and new features of written language.

A few letters of the alphabet can be used to construct or generate a host of little words, as any anagram addict knows, so that establishing those first mental models for letter forms increases the child's power over written language enormously. Being able to write four or five letters directs the child's attention to the features of print and helps him to discover his next acquisitions. Failure to build that initial skill keeps the child poor in knowledge of those units out of which words can be constructed. With a few letters and the will to write the eager child will rapidly extend his repertoire, extracting more knowledge from helpful adults, his books and the printed language in his environment. That guidance is required at some points in this discovery process should be clear from the children's work samples in this book.

Parents will provide children with the writing models with which they, the parents, are familiar. I remember that my mother could not print in lower-case letters. If a parent's education has been limited or in another language he or she may be unable to give the child any writing models or may have learnt only another script such as Urdu or Hebrew or Chinese. Commonly a parent gives the child a capital letter model of his name. Jimmy and Peter have developed capital letter signature. Lois and Kay have used a capital and lower-case mixture, but it is not clear whether they appreciate the capital/lower-case contrast.

Even when provided with a model to copy the child with only a limited range of letters in his writing repertoire has problems in trying to copy his name. Heather and Roberta illustrate this difficulty.

Michael does not think he needs a copy; he can write his name by himself, or at least three letters of it.

aged 5:5

Roberta
ROP(TA

HTET

MID

Heather

Signatures may call attention to the relationships between capital and lower case letters. For Ian, this presented some confusion. He had been taught his name in capitals and he told me that the teacher could not spell his name (in a tone that expressed some pity for her).

'My teacher writes my name like this. She can't even spell'

'My name is really like this.'

aged 5:3

Iain
IAN

Whether the child has to master the conventions of print for English or for Chinese his task appears to be similar in many respects. Charlie has attempted his name twice, once in English and once in Chinese. He has recorded a basic linguistic principle; that one meaning can be 'read out' in different ways in different language codes.

charlie
查上大

The child's own name is a good word to use as a starting point for his insights about written language and teachers have usually acknowledged this. Before the child can reproduce his full name correctly he may have acquired his first written word which he can write without a copy. It may be

Si

This may not be a reversal caused by looking at the wrong end first. It is more likely that the first letter that was remembered was the squiggly 's' and the 'i' was placed second because it was recalled second. Such 'words' and full signatures mark a transition from letters as signs to words as signs.

5. Messages and Meanings

A Code Exists

The two year old will put pencil to paper and scribble for the joy of movement or for the visually satisfying marks that appear. But somewhere between three and five years most children become aware that people make marks on paper purposefully, and in imitation they, the children, may produce

scribble writing

linear mock writing

or mock letters.

The linear scribble that fills the lines of a writing pad has, for the child, all the mystery of an unfamiliar code. It stands for a myriad of possible things but does not convey a particular message. The child seems to say 'I hope I've said something important. You must be able to understand what I've said. What did I write?'

An early linking of sign and meaning is often the child's own name, although at first it will be thought of as 'My sign' rather than letters or words. At the age of 5:5 Sherryl Lyn

aged 5:5

regarded 'S' as her sign and she sat down to write a letter to her grandmother which was virtually variations on an 'S' theme. At this stage children's comments seem to indicate that they have faith in the adult's capacity to read what they have written and Sherryl probably expected her grandmother to know what the writing said.

She completed the activity with an envelope addressed in linear mock writing, imitating the spatial arrangement of the address to the extent of making three horizontal lines.

aged 5:5

In response to all this effort her mother possibly talked about the 'letter' she wrote to grandmother — a different usage of the word 'letter' from the one she will soon have to understand. A few weeks later the linear mock writing persists but more letters have appears — w, c, e (reversed) and the nucleus of D, and c.

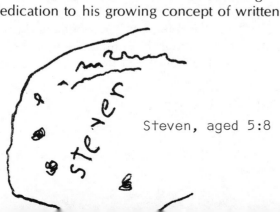

Sherryl Lyn, aged 5:6

Steven mixed scribble writing and linear mock writing. He added his well-developed 'own-sign' or signature and enclosed the product in a sweeping outline. He filled the back of this sheet with sixteen lines of linear mock writing — an amazing dedication to his growing concept of written messages!

Steven, aged 5:8

Bridget, aged 5:1

Peter, aged 5:2

remained locked at this primitive fantasy level ten months later, for he had still not understood that an exact message can be written down. He still believed that marks on paper convey messages which 'you' but not 'I' understand and his lack of progress in writing was paralleled by lack of progress in reading.

Ian, aged 5:8

Developmentally, the pleasure of scribble gives place to the concept that these marks are signals of some as yet unknown meaning. The next step would be to formulate some brief but precise message which the child intends to convey and search for the right signs with which to convey the message. But some children do not demand that an intended message be received. At the age of 5:2 Peter produced a string of letter signs, intermingled with drawing, artistically presented in green and orange crayon. He thought it probably contained an important message after the care he had taken with it, and he delivered it into my hand with the instruction 'Give this to your children, and learn them it,'cause it says a lot of fings!' For a child of 5:2 this work showed promise: it had form, variety, linear stringing of letters and an awareness of the sign concept. But Peter

Ian who was 5:8 drew his animal well but had no confidence to write anything about it. He did manage a tentative 'A' which deserved an enthusiastic reaction from his teacher to boost his progress.

Bridget, like Peter, combines her lettering with her art and 'says a lot of things' but unlike Peter, she rapidly moved to clearer insights of the writing process (see p.49).

6. Phrases and Sentences

Children's *earliest* writing does not record their own thoughts but very soon the ideas that they want to express begin to communicate to adults. The principles of early writing behaviour which have been discussed in earlier chapters can be observed in these first stories.

Message Unknown

At some point beyond the attainment of the sign concept and probably after some letters and single words have been learned the child realises that a whole message can be written down. At the earliest stage of awareness the child hopes that he has written down a message, and that the squiggles he has made do correspond in some way with what he is saying, although he has no basis for establishing this correspondence. At this level his message is a fantasy expressed in print. This can be seen in the following example. I was assured that this message said 'Here is Easter eggs!'

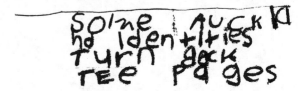

Many of the captions which children copy from their teachers' models have a similar quality. The child has a general idea of the message conveyed but has no way of determining its precise form.

translation: Paul, aged 5:10
watching
a kite fly up
high

Paul may stare dumbly when asked what he has written and think 'I copied the message my teacher wrote, and I suppose it says something but I don't remember exactly what it says.' He is likely to produce a new sentence which paraphrases the first one like 'Look at the kite flying.'

Simple material that is suitable for the child to copy may be hard for him to find around his home, and he may try copying some profound statements, using a newspaper

or magazine,

or an old bus ticket. (Read the fourth line from right to left.)

Sometimes a favourite book seems worth copying and this sample really called for application.

MILKOI MILKOI shouted a voice just
outside Tubby lived there, Mr. Tubby The
teddy bear and his fat little The wife put
her head out of the window.
Two bottles, please, she called. And oh,
milkman you'd better call at the house next door
The little new one, called House-far-One. Mr.
Noddy lives there, and he may want some milk. I
He's just come
That house wasn't there yesterday

At other times a thank you letter may be copied from a mother's script.

The Recurring Principle Again

One new entrant decided that writing was not just lists of letters or lists of words and tried another approach. She thought it might be possible to build a big story by repeating the same words across the line. From a limited repertoire of writing behaviour this child was trying to produce a longer statement. The recurring principle helped her but if she had tried to read what she had written she would probably have been dissatisfied with her product.

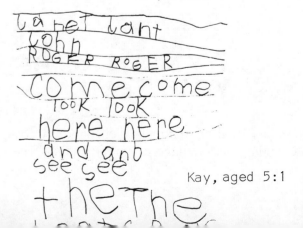

Kay, aged 5:1

One improvement on this strategy would be to repeat some simple word groups with one element varied in each sentence. This device, used in teaching foreign languages, is discovered by some children and leads to efforts like the following example.

Here I Come Said Sue
Here I Come Said Heather
Here I come Said Mother
Here I come Said Father

Speech Written Down

A better way to free oneself from the limitations of the recurring principle is to realise that writing can be speech written down. In the next example Kay clearly realises this because a grammatical error common in the speech of New Entrants has been recorded in 'and I are coming to...' (Perhaps this is intended to be 'too'?)

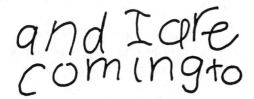

and I are
coming to

The Space Concept

The text in the previous example shows the directional principles correctly applied to groups of words written in two lines but it is doubtful whether the child really acknowledges the value of a space between words. When words are to be combined into word groups *a space must be used to signal the end of one word and the beginning of another.* It is hard for the experienced reader to realise that a space is a signal. Besides signalling the unitary status of what is found between two spaces it also assists visual perception. Readers notice initial and final letters more readily than medial ones, helped by the white space. And as the eye scans lines of print the accuracy of grouping words that make up meaningful phrases is increased by the help the eyes get from the 'spaces between'. Some children take a long time to learn the value of spaces, and this difficulty is often more than just a problem of motor co-ordination. It is a complex mixture of knowing the word segments in the language statement, of knowing the function of the space in the written code, and of having the skill and co-ordination to produce the appropriate spatial record.

The child who is still coping with the difficulties of forming letters may copy a text omitting the spaces.

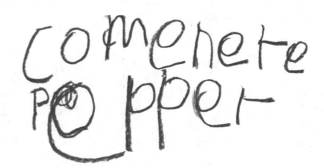

comenete
ppper

The next two examples are letters written to grandmothers. The first letter probably began with word copying but ran off into a string of symbols presented in lines. At this stage the space concept has little significance.

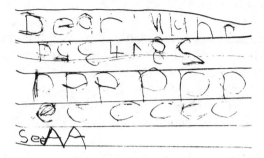

In the second example communication in writing is at a much higher level and the child is producing ideas which she is able to record in word groups. She fully understands that these messages are made up of word units which must be separated by spaces. Despite the obvious control that has been established over the medium of written language the many difficulties of written language are shown by the errors that occur — reversal of the word 'to'; the letter 'b' occurring always in capital form; the word order in 'Love from to Grandma and Grandad'.

The copied and repetitive stories of the 'Here I come said Sue' variety provide practice in making spaces because the words are placed more or less regularly under each other. However, while the idea of the space is becoming established copied stories are likely to include the space and creative stories are likely to omit it. *It is as if the attention can be given either to the visual and spatial aspects of the product or to the language aspects but not to both.* In the following example the child demonstrates control over a number of spatial features such as left to right direction and return sweep, is able to distinguish capital and lower case letters in size, and provides a full stop! But the passage is difficult to read because spaces have been omitted and because one space has crept in where it should not have occurrred. (In the last line the text reads 'the apples on tree').

Stories copied from the blackboard or from another piece of paper are less likely to retain the space, than a child's copy directly under a teacher's script.

Michael, aged 5:9

Teachers' models could exaggerate the space between words when attention to the space is a learning point for a particular pupil. This seems to assist the child to conform to the word-space-word format.

Here is the house and
thats all.

Stephen, aged 5:6

Mother and Sally and
Father are going to
clean their teeth.

Because Lois has now learned to copy a model from the blackboard her teacher is pleased with her effort, even though the letters are poorly formed. This is a more difficult task, but Lois retains the spacing between words very well.

Direction and the Flexibility Principle

When a child is making word lists he sometimes starts in the wrong direction, completes a reversed word, and then corrects himself on the second word listed beneath. However, if by accident he begins a group of words at the right hand side of his page, his behaviour seems to be dominated more by the linear principle of sequencing letters one after the other than by a directional schema for the rules of written language and so he often continues to write from right to left across the page, and even returns down right under his beginning word. Note that the linear sequencing and the return sweep are correct in relation to each other. The starting position is wrong and this has probably initiated a reversal of the whole directional schema.

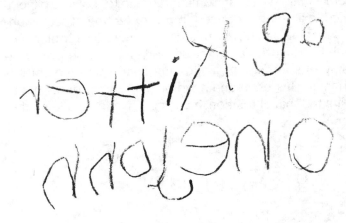

The next example needs translation. It reads 'Barbara and Sherryl Lyn are skipping on the terrace today.' This child had no space concept and is reversing the directional pattern. Correct direction is recovered on two words, 'the', a familiar sequence, and 'today', the last word which may have been perceptually distinctive.

Sherryl Lyn, aged 5:8

One would think that copying from a book would control such directional flexibility. This is not always the case. After the child has gained some control over the directional schema a false start can sometimes lead to a whole page of copied text being produced in mirror writing. It seems unlikely that this can be attributed to a perceptual problem (for which the answer lies in the sensory and intersensory processing of information). Following a false start the child is sequencing his letters and words in appropriate order, maintaining the spatial relationships of each letter to every other letter.

The Generating Principle Again

When the child realises that the word elements can recur in variable patterns he has made considerable progress. He can then produce many new statements in an inventive way. For example,

'I will go to town on the bus'

can be rewritten in at least four different ways without adding or subtracting any words.

I will go on the bus to town.
On the bus I will go to town.
Will I go on the bus to town?
Will I go to town on the bus?

If one omits words many other sentences can be made such as

I go to town.
Will the bus go to town?

Knowledge of a few units of heavy-duty words in English enables the child to generate a variety of products. This is a good point for a teacher to remember when she finds a child who is unable to write stories. The activity may be looked upon as pattern-making.

Perhaps the child can be encouraged to reason like this.

I know some words. (Copying principle)
I can try to write new ones. (Flexibility principle)
I can repeat them. (Recurring principle)
They go one after the other across a line
(Directional principle),
separated by spaces (the Space Concept),
to make new messages (Generating principle).

Children like to feel the mastery that comes from making an extensive statement. By applying the recurring and flexibility principles to sentence construction they can achieve this while their store of words they can write is still small. Some word groups like 'Here is...' and 'I like...' are good for starting several different sentences. In the next three samples the children have discovered these *sentence starters* but were not able to complete the statements.

Hᵉᵣgiₛₚ

David, aged 5:9

Here   Is   ₚ

ₚ ᴅ ₛ ᵢ ₛ ʟ

I   lιke
m ᵧ n ᵂᵉ
ᵥ ᵈ

Heather, aged 5:6

This   is   ᵈ   likes

Craig, aged 5:3

Extensive use of the recurring principle in sentences in this way produces utterances which seem stilted and not very inventive, but the idea of the substitution of words within grammatical structures is a basic feature of language, and the child's discovery of this is a step forward. The recurring principle and the flexibility principle are both used, usually with the sentence starter being repeated and the ending varied. Each of the following sets of sentences was produced by a single child on one day.

Dear Miss Dean

I like the Doll Said Heather
I like the Doll Said Sue
I like the Doll Said Mother

I ILke The zoo
I ILke The DOG
I iIke The CAT
I Iike The Books
I Ikke the school
I IIke The
I Iike The Birds Birds
Books SchoolBirds

aged 5:9

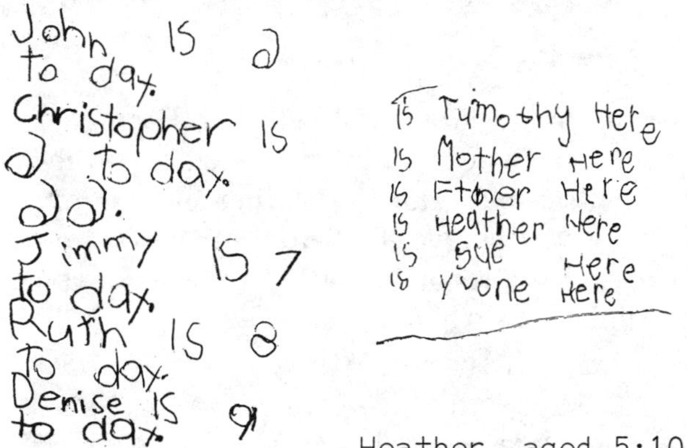

John is a
to day.
Christopher is
a to day.
aa.
Jimmy is 7
to day.
Ruth is 8
to day.
Denise is 9
to day.

Is Timothy Here
Is Mother Here
Is Ftner Here
Is Heather Were
Is Sue Here
Is yvone Here

Heather, aged 5:10

Timothy is helping Heather
Timothy is helping Mother
Timothy is helping Sue
Timothy is helping Rangi

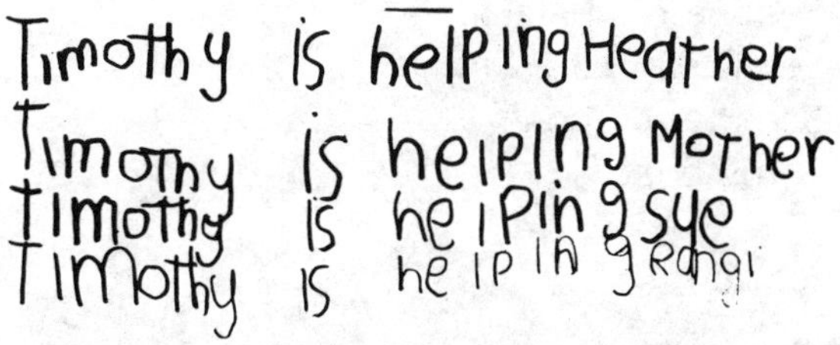

In Steven's example below he was apparently thinking up the repetitive sentence forms 'in his head' and not merely copying from his earlier sentences, because the regular spatial arrangement of the earlier samples is lost.

kerry must
go to his
home Garry
must go t his.
home Ruth
must go
home too
The dog must
go to his   Steven, aged 5:11
hom e

Peter produced the following work samples over several months. He wrote a sentence each day in response to his teacher's request during drawing and writing time. But he kept his very simple standard sentence *for several months*. I have six samples of drawings and sentences before the final breakthrough to a more varied text (which is hard to read).

See the house.	Aged 5:5
See the trees.	Aged 5:6
See the goldfish.	Aged 5:6
See the speedboat.	Aged 5:7
See the big palace.	Aged 5:8
See Robin Hood fight	Aged 5:8
See the me boat.	Aged 5:9
is my boat	Aged 5:10
It is	
let ride in it	

When the child gave up the support of a 'sentence starter' he had both the opportunity of producing more interesting stories and the possibility of making more errors of grammar, meaning, and spacing. As the controlled repetitive sentences which lean heavily on the recurring principle are discarded the teacher may observe many unsuccessful attempts to construct sentences, but *this may well indicate progress*. The child is becoming freed from the rather rigid repetitive sentence structures of his first stories. But now he finds himself trying to control more things than he can manage and the more creative or venturesome he tries to be the more risks he runs. (See Chapter 1 on individual differences.)

Lastly, some errors in word detail occur because the child is trying to write down his speech, using what he knows of letter-sound correspondences in English. In this example the attempt is good, but not quite perfect.

his net was
made of
flaxs and
leaves.

Errors are interesting. They often signal that the child is reaching out to some new facet of written expression, and that he needs help towards some new learning. A little thought will often suggest what knowledge the child used to produce the error, that is, how he tried to find a solution.

More Successful Composition

In an earlier section on Individual Differences I tried to show that errors in children's writing tell a great deal about their stage of progress. There was much thought given to these sentences.

The three bears
going four ther
      walk

Here are for
flowers

Alan and Steven and Debby
went
write down the path...

The next examples are better quality stories produced by those few children who reach this standard of written expression in their first year at school.

It is raining on the kumaras
that the Maoris grew in the
olden days. An aeroplane
flew over head.

Neild ship has
six white
sails.
Neils ship
is a big one
Its name is
The May flower

They are in the dinghy
looking at the pirate ship
they are looking at the treasure

Ken and Betty and Kay are digging in the garden and Mrs. Brown barks and Annie meows. Now the Buckleys have finished their digging in the garden. Now we have a rest. The cat and the dog have a rest too. And Betty goes to cook the tea. Kay and Paul are going to have a bath. Ken has a shower. The Buckleys have tea. Kay and Paul go to brush their teeth. Betty is going to have a shower. Kay and Paul are going to bed. Ken is marking books. Betty is knitting. Ken and Betty go to bed, too.

The cowboy

is riding

his horse with

his hat and

guns he is

riding away

I am playing school
with Kay and Heather and
Paul and Pam, too.
    This is Kay and Linda.
    This is a church for the
Mummys and Daddys, too.
    This is a design.
    This is a balloon.

And what of style? With all the problems of forming letters, spacing words, proceeding in correct directions, getting one's speech and thoughts down on paper, are children influenced by the style of writing in the texts they read? When one little boy was asked to read a basal reader text 'with his finger' he adopted the following directional course.

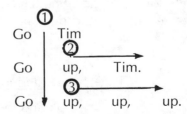

The sentences which he spoke were 'Go, go, go. Tim, Up, Tim. Up, up, up.' It would be difficult to argue that his sentences were any poorer than those of the text he was trying to read, and he seemed to have caught the general idea. In the following example of written expression Kay has adopted the controlled vocabulary principle in that she only uses 13 words to make her statement of 33 running words.

She achieves Seuss-like quality. (She did enjoy reading Dr Seuss.)

here is a house.
Said Betty. yes
Said Paul. yes
Said Ben. I said
yes too. Ben
Said it is a blue
house yes said
Betty. yes said
Paul. I said yes too.

Jenny tried to write a book; her model was the Janet and John basic reading series which used a controlled vocabulary. Her interest lasted for five pages of illustration and text and she included a title for each page. She tended to develop sentences of greater interest and difficulty than the model she was using.

The house.
The house
lives on
The side of
The bank

Mother and father
mother and father
walked home

Page 1 <u>Janet and John</u>
look and look
Come and look
See Janet and John

Page 2 <u>See the boat</u>
The boat
can float.

Page 3 <u>The dog</u>
The dog can
jump and run.

Page 4 <u>The house.</u>
The house
lives on
The side of
The bank.

Page 5 <u>Mother and father</u>
Mother and father
walked home.

The next example requires some effort to decode the message. It is an original story which owes a lot to the Billy Goats Gruff and its villain is a 'dwharf'. But there are two very interesting features in the layout of this story. The minor one relates to the directional principles. A left to right ordering of letters within words, and of words within sentences is achieved, and the return down left is consistently maintained. The space concept is usually included and sentences end with fullstops, although the new sentences which start with 'and' do not begin with a capital letter. However, the *story* begins in the top *right-hand* corner, and moves from there to the *top left-hand corner*. It then proceeds from left blocks to right blocks down the page. The left to right sequencing did not transfer from the letters, and words, to the blocks of ideas. These blocks of ideas are of even greater interest. Perhaps the child is merely thinking about a story book, and trying to convey the idea of pages each containing a small segment of the story. Possibly she has demonstrated a primitive awareness of the principle of paragraphing.

Finally two examples from two space-conscious boys of six and a half years. Which is making the better progress? What are the learning hurdles facing the child who wrote the poorer sample? One was written by an English boy from a professional home and one is by a Samoan boy.

Who is walking on my Stairs. said the old dwharf.

I am said a voice and my lttle babies and my children well I will come up to eat your baby und your children und you up come und eat us

and the dwharf cume up. to eut us.

and theBilly goat went away.

But the people und the baby and the girl ran intothe dwharfs home. uNu Billy goat clime up + he stairs.

und the people undbaby went away

und the Billy goat push the dwhart in to the pond.

und they were happy

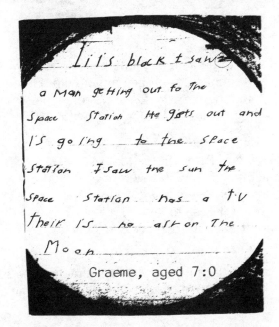

Iiis black t saw a Man getting out fo The Space Station He gets out and I's going to the space Station I saw the sun the Space Station has a tv their I's no ast on The Moon

Graeme, aged 7:0

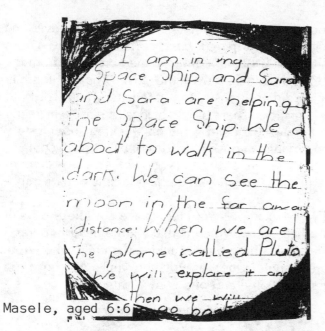

I am in my
Space Ship and Sara
and Sara are helping
the Space Ship. We a
about to walk in the
dark. We can see the
moon in the far away
distance. When we are
the plane called Pluto
We will explore it and
then we will go back

Masele, aged 6:6

There seems to be a great learning distance between the repetitive early sentences all beginning with 'Here is...' or 'This is a...' and these examples of written expression. And yet, when the first attempts of variety within structure are noted,

I am playing at Peters home today
I am playing tennis with Peter on the court today
I am playing at Peters home today
Peter is at my house today too
Bruce and russel are playing at russels
house today

it is not so very far to these flexible sentences structures, packed with descriptive commentary, written by an eleven year old.

By Blue Lake on the north side is a tiny village. At the wharf are moored many boats and just above the long sandy beach is a white two-storey house...

Dissatisfied, she tries again to re-write her introduction.

Down a rocky hillside by the clear blue waters of Blue Lake is a tiny village. In this village is a special family which this story is about...

What these efforts have in common with her earlier work at 4:11 (see p.29) is mastery of the generating and flexibility principles.

The most difficult step in the entire process is taken when the child leaves the security of the repetitive structure, tries to become more flexible, varies the form of his statement, and uses elements within these structures flexibly and interchangeably. This is comparatively easy for the child who already speaks with a rich vocabulary and a variety of sentence forms. All his teachers need to do is *to reward his efforts*. The child who speaks English as a second language can only apply the generating and flexibility principles in limited ways to those few syntactic structures he already knows. His progress depends very much upon his learning about the language, and particularly the grammatical alternatives allowed in English. The first child has only to transform his oral language skills for the new task of writing language. The second child has to learn more about language, its vocabulary and structures, as he learns to write.

7. Application

The principles described in this book can now be briefly summarised and readers are invited to explore some further examples of children's work perhaps discussing in groups the features they display. At the end of the chapter is a Rating Technique for observing and rating the level of a child's performance in the first six months of instruction. This could be applied to some of the samples. A technique for taking an inventory of Writing Vocabulary as a reliable rating of first year progress is also described. For slow progress readers such an inventory has a dual purpose. It indicates the severe limitations on the vocabulary that they know, and it provides a core vocabulary around which special reading material can be constructed. They can then gradually add new words into the sentence contexts which they already control.

1. The Sign Concept

This is an early and easy concept. A sign carries a message. But problems arise when children fail to move beyond the stage of producing signs. At age 5:2 Peter produced a string of letter signs which he thought might contain some important message, but at 6:0 Peter was still in the sign stage and had not progressed to producing primitive messages! (See p. 50).

2. The Message Concept

The child at this stage realises that the messages that he speaks can be written down. At an early stage he hopes optimistically that what he has written down does correspond with what he is saying, although he has no basis whatever for establishing this correspondence.

3. The Copying Principle

Some letters, some words and some word groups must be imitated or copied in a slow and laborious way to establish the first units of printing behaviour. But one frequently observes how quickly the child tires of a copying task and how he 'descends' to the easier task of inventing forms for himself. Careful copying is a check on wayward inventing, but inventing is a quicker way to new discoveries.

4. The Flexibility Principle

Left to experiment with letter forms children will create a variety of new symbols by repositioning or decorating the standard forms. This enables them to explore the limits within which each letter form may be varied and still retain its identity. When is a sign not a language sign? When is a sign a new sign?

Many of the 'errors' in children's creative writing at this early stage must be regarded as indicators of this flexibility which is essential for the complex learning to be mastered. Can you turn a letter around? The answer is usually no. Can you change the letter order around? Again the answer is no. Can you begin on the right-hand side of the page, or at the bottom? The answer is no. The limits set by the conventions of the printer's code can be discovered by such explorations. Verbal explanation of such things is tedious and difficult. It is probably easier to 'catch on' to the rule.

There is one other feature of the flexibility principle observable in the examples. While the child is exploring the limits of some new feature of writing, responses which are already adequate may recover their flexibility (become disorganized, in other words) and letters or words may reappear in wrong positions, wrong forms and wrong orders. Thus new difficulties can produce a regression in recently learned responses (which is true in other aspects of development). It is as if the old habits recover their flexibility to admit the new learning before settling to a new organization of the habitual response. Such flexibility may be of central importance in the early stages of any complex learning.

5. The Inventory Principle

Until I began observing five year olds closely I had no idea that they took stock of their own learning so systematically, that they spontaneously made lists of what they knew or that they arranged or consciously ordered their learning, as some of the examples of structured inventories suggest.

6. The Recurring Principle

The tendency to repeat an action has the obvious advantage of helping in the establishment of quick, habitual response patterns and it probably produces pleasant feelings of competence. But it makes an even greater contribution to the child's progress when he realises that the same elements can recur in variable patterns (as in the alphabetic principle).

7. The Generating Principle

An easy way to extend one's repertoire is to know some elements, and to know some rules for combining or arranging these elements. One can then produce many new statements in an inventive way. This seems to suit the young learner better than the laborious technique of copying. It is facilitated by the flexibility principle, and by the recurring principle.

8. The Directional Principles

Language is written in two-dimensional space according to a set of printer's conventions which the adult writer or reader takes for granted. For correct behaviour to occur the child must start at the top left, move from left to right, and return to a left hand position under the starting point, establishing a top to bottom progression. A *pattern* of appropriate movements is required. Critical for appropriate directional responding is the starting point. The young child trying to locate himself on a page of paper might choose any starting point. If he happens to choose a top left starting position it is difficult to move in the wrong direction. If left and right starting points are frequently alternated the child may become confused about directional behaviour.

Research results suggest that there are four segments to the directional pattern of movements used in written English and that these are mastered after about six months at school by many children, and by that time the sequence is learnt as a total plan of action. Until some control has been gained over the directional principles the flexibility principle will be evident in the variety of approaches to print that children can devise. And lapses from consistency within the pattern of movements might be expected to recur as new difficulties are encountered.

9. Reversing the Directional Pattern

It is common to find mirror writing at this stage, and the facility that young children show with this suggests that some rather simple explanation must exist. It is possible to find a child who wants to start at the bottom of a page and work upwards, or who wants to write down the left hand side from top to bottom before making a second list. However, it is more common to find mirror writing. Frequently this occurs because the child has selected a starting point towards the right-hand edge of the page. Perhaps he senses that he will run off the page if he moves from left to right and so reverses his entire pattern of directional movement. He may correct himself after one line. But if the movement sequence is well established he may reverse the whole sequence and produce mirror script. This happens even when he is copying text from a book (p. 56). Mirror writing at this stage is a lapse in the sense of body in space as it relates to the page of a book rather than a lapse in visual perception. The two rapidly become linked so that one month after entry to school a child closes her eyes tight, makes letter shapes in the air and claims 'I can see my finger writing.' All difficulties with directional principles are not accounted for by reversals, but many could be readily overcome simply by guidance as to correct starting position. (A 'green light' adhesive sticker can be placed and removed as needed.)

10. The Contrastive Principle

It is a feature of language that contrasts can be made between units at several levels. It was a surprise to me to find children playfully creating contrasts between shapes, meanings, sounds and word patterns. The examples come only from those children who made rapid progress in learning to read, but they are further evidence of the urge, not only to explore, but also to order one's knowledge.

11. The Space Concept

When the child passes from writing single words to writing words in groups some new problems arise. A space must be used to signal the end of one word and the beginning of another. Some children take a long time to adapt to this requirement. They may not even hear the 'word' as a segmented part of their spoken sentence. They may not understand the function of the space in print.

12. Page and Book Arrangement

A child may know the directional principles and operate within them. But he encounters new difficulties when he runs out of page and cannot fit his word or his sentence on the line or on a page. In an economical way he tends to fill the left-over spaces with his left-over utterances, ignoring at that moment the directional principles. The new complexities introduced in this situation upset established responses to letter orientation and letter order.

13. The Abbreviation Principle

Although not a very significant principle at this level of progress the abbreviation principle was understood by some of the better readers in this study before their sixth birthdays. (See p. 38) It is an important and advanced achievement because the child who intentionally uses an abbreviation probably understands that words are constructed out of letters and that the letters of abbreviations 'stand for' words and could be filled out or expanded into full forms. Letter and word concepts are established and their interrelationships understood.

has
has
he
got
egros

aged 5:8

What does this child know about
our written code?

A Rating Technique for Observing Early Progress

To estimate the level of a young child's written expression in the first six months of instruction take three samples of his written work on consecutive days, or over a period. The child's behaviour must develop in each of three areas and he should receive a rating for each aspect of the writing task. This is an arbitrary scale and should be taken only as a rough guide to a child's instruction needs.

LANGUAGE LEVEL: Record the number of the highest level of linguistic organization used by the child.
1.   Alphabetic (letters only)
2.   Word (any recognisable word)
3.   Word Group (any two word phrase)
4.   Sentence (any simple sentence)
5.   Punctuated story (of two or more sentences)
6.   Paragraphed story (two themes)

MESSAGE QUALITY: Record the number below for the best description of the child's sample.
1. He has a concept of signs (uses letters, invents letters, uses punctuation.)
2. He has a concept that a message is conveyed (ie he tells you a message but what he has written is not that message).
3. A message is copied, and he knows more or less what that message says.
4. Repetitive, independent use of sentence patterns like 'here is a ...'
5. Attempts to record own ideas, mostly independently.
6. Successful composition.

DIRECTIONAL PRINCIPLES: Record the number of the highest rating for which there is no error in the sample of the child's writing.

1. No evidence of directional knowledge.
2. Part of the directional pattern is known
   Either   Start top left
   Or   Move left to right
   Or   Return down left
3. Reversal of the directional pattern (right to left and/or return down right). A sample with one lapse should be rated at this level.
4. Correct directional pattern.
5. Correct directional pattern and spaces between words.
6. Extensive text without any difficulties of arrangement and spacing of text.

	A Language Level	B Message Quality	C Directional Principles
Not yet Satisfactory	1 - 4	1 - 4	1 - 4
Probably Satisfactory	5 - 6	5 - 6	5 - 6

An Inventory of Writing Vocabulary for Rating Progress

A test of writing vocabulary, constructed Susan E. Robinson (1973) was included in the test battery of her research on predicting early reading progress. Hildreth (1963) and de Hirsch et al (1966) had suggested that writing behaviour was a good indicator of a child's knowledge of letters, and of left to right sequencing behaviour. In writing words letter by letter the child must recall not only the configuration but also the details. Children's written texts are a good source of information about a child's visual discrimination of print for as the child learns to print words, hand and eye support and supplement each other to organize the first visual discriminations.

A test was constructed where the child was encouraged to write down all the words he knew how to write, starting with his own name and including basic vocabulary and words personal to the child. This simple test was both reliable (ie a child tended to score at a similar level when retested two weeks later) and valid in the sense that it had a high relationship with word reading scores.

Spearman rank correlations of test re-test scores were obtained for two administrations of writing vocabulary of not less than a week and not more than two weeks apart. For 34 children aged 5:6 the correlation was 0.97. A validity check was made by correlating writing vocabulary scores and scores on Clay's word reading test for 50 children aged 5:6. A Pearson product moment correlation coefficient of 0.82 was obtained. This was very similar to the correlation Malmquist (1961, p 153). found between a beginning reader's ability to read alphabet letters and his ability to write alphabet letters (r. 0.81). Malmquist concluded that 'the development of both writing and reading ability... evidently follow each other rather closely.' (Robinson, 1973).

The distribution of scores changes markedly when a group of 5½ year olds is compared with two groups of six year olds in the following graph.

There is probably a high degree of interdependence between reading words and writing words. Writing ability and word reading ability may both be the result of many kinds of experience with letters, numbers, words, stories, and drawings which have enabled the child to learn many things about print. It should not be assumed from this study that success in the first years of learning to read would be assured by simply teaching children to write words.

ADMINISTRATION: The procedure followed was to give the child a clean piece of paper and a pencil and then the experimenter (E) said

'I want to see how many words you can write. Can you write your name?'

If the child said 'No', E asked him if he knew any single letter or two letter words.

'Do you know how to write is? to? I? or a'?
Usually when the child did not know his name he knew very few other words.

If the child said 'Yes', then E said

'Write your name for me'.

When the child had finished E said

'Good. Now think of all the words you know how to write and write them all down for me'.

Usually the child started to write words of his own accord. When he stopped writing, or when he needed prompting, words were suggested that he might know how to write.

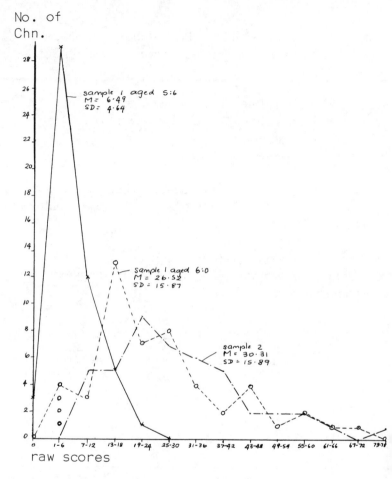

No. of Chn.

sample 1 aged 5:6
M = 6·49
SD = 4·64

sample 1 aged 6:0
M = 26·52
SD = 15·87

sample 2
M = 30·31
SD = 15·89

raw scores

Distribution of scores on an open-ended writing vocabulary test.

'Do you know how to write I or a?'
'Do you know how to write is or to?'
(And so on through a list of basic vocabulary that the child

would have met in his reading books — the, in, at, am, on, up, and, go, look, come, here, this, me, he, we, mother, father, car, for). This was continued until the child's writing vocabulary was exhausted or after ten minutes. Very able children needed little prompting but sometimes a category of words was suggested.

'Do you know how to write your number words like the word one?'

'Do you know how to write your colour words like the word red?'

'Do you know how to write your days of the week like the word Monday?'

'Do you know how to write your months of the year like the word May?'

'Do you know how to write any other names of children like Bill, Peter?'

SCORING: Each word completed accurately was marked as correct. If the child accidentally wrote a word that was correct but read it as another word or did not know what it was it was scored an error. Words written in mirror image were scored as correct only if the child actually wrote them in the correct sequence. Progressions such as look, looks, looked, looking, and sat, fat, mat, hat, were allowed as separate words.

ATTAINMENT: Some children could not reproduce their own names. Half of the children aged 5:6 could not write more than four to seven words. Only four children at this age wrote more than 13 words. The results for children aged 6:0 were far higher, the mean score for two samples being 26 and 29. Even with the ten-minute time limit the writing vocabulary of able children was by no means exhausted. One child wrote 79 words accurately in ten minutes. The graph shows how one group of children aged

5:6 (solid line) had changed in scoring by six years (light dashed). A second group of six year olds (dashes and dots) were also widely distributed on this skill.

A developmental record of a child's progress may be kept by taking an inventory of writing vocabulary at several points in time — at entry, after six months and after one year. In the following examples the progress of individual children is noticeable even though they are at different levels of attainment. (Compare Ross and Nicola for example.)

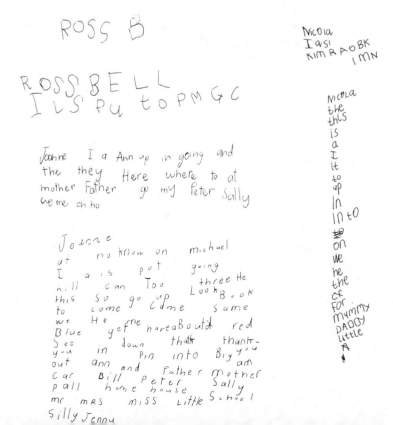

8. Early Writing: Some Theoretical Links with Reading

Introduction

For children who learn to write at the same time as they learn to read, writing plays a significant part in the early reading progress. Some reading instruction programmes have stressed the importance of early writing (Spaulding & Spaulding, 1969) and others such as i.t.a. have claimed that reading instruction assists children to become fluent writers of English sooner than other programmes (Downing, 1964). Especially when an analytic approach is taken to early reading instruction and sentences are analysed into words which are further analysed into letters or sounds, then writing provides a complementary synthetic experience where letters are built into words which make up sentences (Clay, 1972). The child who writes a simple statement like

I   am   Belinda

demonstrates a mastery of some basic hierarchical relationships between letters, words and messages. There is strong evidence from a recent research study which supports this argument. Robinson (1973) using a large battery of tests and relating these to longitudinal records of reading progress between 5½ and 6½ years found that her measure of writing vocabulary (see p 67) was such a good predictor of reading progress in some New Zealand schools that it dwarfed the significance of other test variables previously described as important by Clay (1972).

Remedial programmes for severely retarded readers have usually stressed writing as an aid to reading especially where the child has motor inco-ordination or visual perception problems.

- Marion Munro

For teaching children who had trouble in learning to read Marion Munro held motor responses to be very important partly because they are easily observed and partly because they force the child to make different motor responses to different sensory characteristics and thereby reinforce the visual-auditory learning with memories of motor movements.

- Samuel Orton

Orton drew attention to the fact that children who have a difficulty in re-picturing a word with correct sequence of letters, of sounds or of units of movement can be helped by finger movements.

- Grace Fernald

Fernald considered that dependence on visual methods in teaching reading made it impossible for some children to use their particular strengths and learn by other methods. She believed that a large percentage of children with partial or extreme disability in learning to read need to approach reading through the kind of analysis that is required to write language.

The child seems to derive a sense of mastery when he writes a word which is recognised by an adult. To achieve this he had to attend to the detail of the letters he wrote, and the principle of correct letter order. Far more important *he had to organise his own behaviour into an appropriate sequence of actions.*

If he was copying he had to co-ordinate the movements of his eyes, as he visually scanned the word, with movement patterns of his hand in reproducing it. And if he was writing the word from memory he had to mentally scan his memories of that word and translate these *in sequence* into movement patterns for writing it. In both activities he was directing his own behaviour to analyse words in detail and in sequence. He was calling upon those areas of the brain which are responsible for synthesising collections of information. He had learnt

- how to visually analyse words, and
- what to study in a word so as to be able to reproduce it, and
- how to organize his own actions to achieve this writing goal.

Yet some authors would maintain that reading would be tedious if it were tied to such slow analysis and some authors of reading programmes have tried to protect children from the boredom of too much writing. There is no doubt that in some classrooms writing is merely a busy work.

If a child knows how to scan, how to study a word in order to reproduce it, and how to organize his writing of that word he has the skills to deal with the detail of print. It is probable that early writing serves to organize the visual analysis of print. In addition the child's work provides us with objective evidence of what he has learnt.

- We can observe the organized behaviour in word-writing.
- We can assume functional organization in the brain from observing the correct copying of a word carried out in an appropriate sequence.
- We can assume the capacity to synthesise information from several sources as we see a child write a new word without a copy.

My aim in early writing instruction would be to provide many interesting activities to establish and stabilise these strategies for analysing words. I would assume that they would then remain in the child's behaviour repertoire if called into action from time to time. In other words practice in writing could be critical at an early learning stage and of much less value *for reading progress* once the basic visual scanning and memory strategies were established.

A Behaviour Programme or System

An eminent Russian neuro-psychologist has described how a study of injuries to the brain provided him with a theory of complex brain functioning in speech and writing (Luria, 1970). Luria stresses that particular zones in the brain are responsible for the synthesis into a coherent whole of collections of information from memory and from different senses. Every complex form of behaviour depends on the joint operation of several areas located in different zones of the brain. It is a combination of cues 'out there', of memories, and of expectations of what might happen next which enables the person to perform complex actions, to understand the complex grammar of a sentence spoken to him, or the intricacy of a mathematical solution.

If we recall how difficult it is to start to move one's leg if the leg has become numb this focusses us on the fact that during each moment of a complicated movement, the position of a limb is different and the brain has to receive messages from the muscles and joints and has to send impulses in the right order to that limb. That is the inner aspect of the complicated movement.

But a second aspect of voluntary movement is its relationship to the spatial field. The movement has to be precisely directed towards a certain point in space. The analysis of space beyond one's own body is done in a part of the brain different from that part controlling the movement. If a person cannot correctly evaluate the spaces that he moves in, then voluntary movements of his limb will be problematical. Luria poetically describes a skilled movement as a kinetic melody of inter-changeable links, likening it to the complexity of a musical composition.

Luria analyses the complex ability of writing language.
• One region of the brain is responsible for the first step of analysing words into their individual sounds.
• Another separate area of the brain is responsible for the articulation of speech sounds.
• The next step towards writing the word is coding the sound units into the units of writing, that is, the sounds into letters. This step calls into play still another part of the brain in the visual and spatial zones.
• The mental process of writing a word entails a further skill; putting the letters in the proper sequence to form the word. This involves a large area of the brain as a whole. This is the matter of expressing thoughts and ideas.

Luria suggests that this is why people commonly pronounce an unfamiliar word before writing it and in the case of an unfamiliar name ask a person to spell it. One of his co-workers conducted an experiment with Russian elementary school children to demonstrate the linking of speech and writing. The children were instructed to hold their mouths open or to immobilise their tongues with their teeth while they wrote. In these circumstances, unable to articulate the words, the children made six times as many spelling mistakes.

Adults find it difficult to analyse the problems of very young children as these children approach the task of learning about written language. Luria possibly provides an explanation for such difficulty. He has concluded that training and practice change the organisation of the brain's activity so that the brain comes to perform an accustomed task without having to analyse this task. That is to say, the final performance of the task may be based on a network of cells in the brain which is quite different from the network that was called on originally when a performance required the help of the analytic processes.

Visual Analysis and Eye Movements

In a recently published bibliography on visual perception and its relation to reading Magdelen Vernon described how children gradually develop the capacity to perceive forms, their spatial orientation and their sequence. Most children are adept at the perception of simple forms when they enter school but have difficulty in analysing complex forms. She finds some disagreement in the literature as to whether children's visual perception on entry to school is sufficiently mature for them to identify letter shapes but those who are superior in the perception of simple forms usually learn to read more quickly.

How do we recognise objects and pictures which we see? Photography of eye movements has shown very clearly that it takes time for adults to scan a complicated object or picture and that there is something systematic about how we will explore this with our eye movements. If an object is small and distant we see it at a glance. If it is close and large our eyes move across the object or picture in some scanning pattern. Noton and Stark (1971) believe that their experiments support three main conclusions about the visual recognition of objects and pictures. First we have a memory of an object or symbol that we have seen before and that memory is a collection of memories of the features of that object or symbol. Second, the features of an object which one remembers are those that yield the most information; that is, those which make it clearly distinguishable from other objects. Thirdly other memories record the shifts of attention we have to make to pass from one feature to the other. These shifts may be actual eye movements if the object is large or merely shifts of attention as the mind focusses on one feature after the other in a preferred order resulting in what might be called a scanning pass. Shifts of attention apparently replace eye movements in attending to objects small enough to be viewed with single fixation. The subject's attention moves around the picture even when his eyes appear to be fixed at a certain point.

Norton and Stark put forward the following explanation to the question 'How do we recognise things?' As a subject views an object for the first time and becomes familiar with it, he scans it with his eyes and develops a scan path for it. During this time he lays down the memory traces of the features which records both the visual features and the motor activity. When he subsequently encounters the same object again, he recognises it by 'watching' with his memory. He matches the successive features and carries out the intervening eye movements, as directed by the features.

Attending to Features of Print

Child psychologists in USSR have paid close attention to the development of voluntary actions in pre-school children. As the young child grows considerable changes can be seen in his ability to initiate, plan and carry out activities in play or in self-care. In a book entitled *Attention, Arousal and the Orientation Reaction* a British psychologist, Lynn, has related these Russian theories to what has been noted in Western child development, and claims that 'investigations convincingly show that the child's ability to act in a voluntary and efficient manner is dependent upon the development of orientation to the task with which he has to cope.'

When the task is a new one orienting involves investigatory actions which explore the situation to discover its nature, and its scope. A simple task like pressing a range of push-buttons, moving a toy car through a maze or copying a letter-like symbol has to be attended to in this way.

When the task is more familiar one can sometimes observe the child making anticipatory movements as though he were rehearsing in some reduced way the movement he is about to carry out. This is also orienting activity and occurs with a partially familiar task.

And when the child has learned a particular action rather well orientation to the task takes place on a mental plane and is limited to a visual examination of the situation. Perhaps the brain circuits needed to carry out the action are alerted and readied by this attending behaviour, which is what Lynn refers to as arousal. Such changes in approach to a problem vary with its newness or familiarity.

Other changes in the method of approach to a problem have been observed in children at different ages. In the youngest children approaching a new and complex task investigatory actions may seem to have no system and appear to be disorganized. Slightly older children demonstrate a little more system in their exploratory movements of body, hands, fingers and eyes. Then there is a stage when more visual exploration accompanies hand movements. Finally a stage is reached when the child can use visual exploration alone to 'sense' 'imagine' or 'anticipate' the movements that would explore the task.

In summary, then, efficient performance of a motor activity necessitates
- attending and orienting to the task,
- investigating or exploring its dimensions, and
- self-direction in sequencing and carrying out a set of movements.

Once these behaviours have been developed the performance of a task is no longer dependent upon such detailed observing of the situation. The orienting movements are reduced to essentials. And by way of a bonus the strategies which had to be learned in order to, say, write the first one or two words can now be applied to a whole class of similar circumstances; to all other words.

The child's first steps in writing language described in this book can be readily analysed in this way. Letter formation, directional behaviour and even the breakaway from stereotyped sentences to creative statements might be traced in these terms.

What is of greater interest here is what such learning would contribute to reading progress. If a child was already efficient at visual exploration he would very quickly learn to orient to printed words or letters without needing to learn how to explore visually. So, for the advanced child only the directional conventions of printed English need be established.

But for most five year old children who are still developing the skills of visual exploration and who learn visual perception with the support of hand and finger movements early writing activities would presumably have the function of encouraging the development of those visual exploration behaviours so necessary in reading. The function of early writing experience would be to develop the visual attending or orienting behaviours needed for attending to the detail of written language. If these are learned in one or two particular situations (a few words and a few simple sentence patterns) they may then be applied to a whole class of similar situations in later reading.

There are beginning reading programmes which assume that all children are efficient at visual analysis. The hand and finger co-ordination required for early writing is seen to be tedious and difficult for the young child and so writing activities are minimised. This contradicts a large body of careful experimentation and a number of important insights known to authors of programmes on remedial reading. The child who fails in reading is almost always a child who has little or no writing vocabulary. This probably means that he is unable to analyse printed forms in any but disorganized ways.

One frequently sees a statement which implies 'How can the child write words until he can read them?' The foregoing analysis suggests the opposite point of view. 'How can the child read words until he can direct his attention in systematic ways?' If a writing programme fosters the development of self-direction in locating, exploring and producing appropriate analysis of printed forms then one is tempted to say 'How can any child who is not exceptional learn to read until he can write some words?'

One caution must be included here. Orienting, and the self-direction of a set of movements is not the same as having that behaviour organised for you. The passive movement of the child's hands through a set of movements is a slow way to teach him but must be resorted to for the poorly co-ordinated child. And learning from verbal directions is a stage that follows those discussed above. It therefore seems that the emphasis in an early writing programme should be on self-directed activity rather than on passive guidance or on verbal direction from the teacher.

Writing and Directional Behaviour

Adults seldom find it hard to distinguish left from right but children and animals sometimes have difficulty. Corballis and Beale have studied this problem and suggest that the trouble stems from the fact that our nervous system has bilateral symmetry. For example we can get similar messages from both our left and our right sides. In their article these authors discuss the implications of this for reading and writing.

The direction of reading and writing seems to be merely a matter of convention. About A.D. 1500 there were as many scripts written and read from right to left as there were written and read from left to right. With the expansion of European culture in the centuries that followed, left to right scripts came to predominate. Even today, however, Hebrew and Arabic are written from right to left. In all cultures so far tested the majority of people are right-handed and right eye dominant, so that there appears to be no cause or relation between handedness and eye dominance on the one hand and the direction of reading and writing on the other. Some early scripts, known as boustrophedon (literally 'ox-turning', or the ploughing of alternate furrows in opposite directions), consisted of alternating left-to-right and right-to-left lines.

The authors believe that one can only make a decision between left or right directions or positions by using some asymmetrical response. Some simple forms of this would be a response like a preference for one hand, or a left to right eye scan, or a tilt of the head to one side, which was behaviour observed in some pigeons who learnt an asymmetrical response. This is all the asymmetry that is needed for the most complex mirror-image discrimination.

One might assume then that the young child trying to attend to print would be assisted in learning the directional rules of written English by establishing either or both of two asymmetrical responses. These are
a) The predominant use of one hand, and either would suffice.
b) The practice of left to right directional sequence required in writing his name, and some other simple words or sentences.

In Summary

The theories and experiments quoted above suggest many links between early writing activities and the skills needed in learning to read.

Some of the skills and concepts that can be learned are these:
- How to attend and orient to printed language.
- How to organize one's exploratory investigation of printed forms.
- How to tell left from right.
- How to visually analyse letters and words.
- What to study in a word so as to be able to reproduce it.
- How to direct one's behaviour in carrying out a sequence of movements needed in writing words and sentences.

In a recent analysis of the effects of a writing system on reading Gillooly (1973) concluded that the influence was important when the child was learning to read but that 'once reading skill has been acquired writing system characteristics no longer exert any appreciable influence on the act of reading.' The implications of these conclusions are simple. The researcher must seek to understand more clearly the interplay in learning between early writing and early reading. And the class teacher who has to introduce young children to written language may expect to find that the sensitive observation of early writing behaviour provides some of the information she will need to individualize instruction in reading and to monitor a child's progress in learning some basic concepts about print.

References

Arkadey, A.G. and Braverman, E.M., *Teaching Computers to Recognise Patterns,* Academic Press, London, 1967.

Clay, Marie M., 'Emergent Reading Behaviour'. Unpubl. Ph. D. thesis, University of Auckland Library, 1966.

Clay, Marie M., *Reading: The Patterning of Complex Behaviour,* Heinemann Educ. Books, Auckland, 1972.

Clay, Marie M., *The Early Detection of Reading Difficulties: A Diagnostic Survey* (with a test booklet, *Sand*), Heinemann Educational Books, Auckland, 1972.

Corballis, M.C. and Beale, I.L., 'On telling left from right.' *Scientific American,* 96, 1971.

De Hirsch, Katrina, Jansky, J. and Longford, W.S., *Predicting the Failing Reader,* Harper and Row, New York, 1966.

Downing, J.A., *The i.t.a. Reading Experiment,* University of London Institute of Education, 1964.

Diringer, D., *Writing,* Thames and Hudson, London, 1962.

Fernald, Grace, *Remedial Techniques in Basic School Subjects,* McGraw-Hill, New York, 1943.

Gillooly, W.B., 'The influence of writing-system characteristic on learning to read.' *Reading Research Quarterly, 8,2,* 1973, 167-199.

Hildreth, G., 'Early writing as an aid to reading.' *Elementary English,* 40, 1964, 15-20.

Holbrook, D., *Children's Writing: A Sampler For Student Teachers,* University Press, Cambridge, 1967.

Luria, A.R., *Higher Cortical Functions in Man,* Tavistock, London, 1966.

Luria, A.R., 'The functional organization of the brain.' *Scientific American,* March, 1970.

Mason, Stella E. (Ed.), *Signs, Signals, and Symbols,* Methuen, London, 1963.

Monro, Marion, *Children Who Cannot Read,* University of Chicago Press, Chicago, 1932.

Noton, D., and Stark, L., 'Eye movements and visual perception.' *Scientific American,* 1971.

Orton, Samuel, *Reading, Writing and Speech Problems in Children,* Norton, New York, 1937.

Piaget, J., and Inhelder, Barbel, *The Child's Conception of Space,* Routledge and Kegan Paul, London, 1956.

Reid, Jessis, 'Learning to think about reading.' *Educational Research,* 9, 56-62, 1966.

Robinson, Susan M., 'Predicting Early Reading Progress.' Unpubl. M.A. thesis, University of Auckland Library, 1973.

Taylor, Joy, *Reading and Writing in the First School,* George Allen and Unwin, London, 1973.

Index